LEW WELCH

HOW I WORK AS A POET
& Other Essays / Plays / Stories

Edited by Donald Allen

Grey Fox Press
Bolinas 1973

SBN: 0-912516-06-2 (paper)
      0-912516-07-0 (cloth)

Library of Congress catalog card number: 73-84119

Book Design by Zoe Brown

Composition by W.O. Turner

Cover photograph: Lew Welch as the Cop in Robert Nelson's
film *The Great Blondino*; photo credit Jack Fulton

Grey Fox Press books are distributed by Book People,
2940 Seventh Street, Berkeley, California 94710

Contents

Editor's Note

"How I Work as a Poet," the title piece of this collection, is a talk Lew Welch gave at Reed College on 30 March 1971 — a few weeks before he disappeared in the Sierra Nevada foothills. It is the latest and the fullest of his several attempts at a statement of his poetics that has survived. Another attempt, which overlaps slightly, is "Language Is Speech," a start on a textbook for a course in poetry; it grew out of his experiences teaching the University of California Extension Poetry Workshop between 1965 and 1970.

"Manifesto: Bread vs. Mozart's Watch" was written for Ralph Gleason's *San Francisco Chronicle* column on the occasion of the big "Free Way Reading" he gave with Gary Snyder and Philip Whalen on 11 June 1964. In 1967 and 1968, at the height of the Haight-Ashbury period, he contributed "A Moving Target Is Hard to Hit" to the Communication Company, and "Greed" and "Final City / Tap City" to the *San Francisco Oracle*. Then, later in 1968, when Paul Krassner of *The Realist* wanted to include the latter essay in "The Digger Papers," Welch rewrote it retaining only the first section from the earlier version. The reviews of books by Richard Brautigan and Philip Whalen were written for William Hogan and the *San Francisco Chronicle*.

In 1963, while batching at Forks of Salmon, in Siskiyou County, he attempted a short play but abandoned it after a few pages. During the next three years he went on to write his "Leather Prunes," which he performed brilliantly as "One-Man Plays" at the San Francisco Museum of Art in October of 1966. "Thirty Thirty" was written as a birthday gift for Joanne Kyger in 1964. He preserved a copy but seems not to have regarded it as a "Leather Prune."

Lew Welch first met Jack Kerouac when he came to San Francisco in late 1959; they soon became friends and in November, with Albert Saijo, he drove him back to New York City. They had many discussions of the problems of writing novels, and in Northport Kerouac demonstrated how he wrote on a long teletype roll rigged to his typewriter. Very much turned on, Welch devoted the better part of 1960 to work on two novels, but in the end they failed to hold his interest and he abandoned them. "The Man Who Played Himself" and "The Late Urban Love of Peter Held" come from one of these episodic works. "Coda" is a fragment from another novel he was writing in the late sixties.

Grateful acknowledgment is made to Reed College for permission to print "How I Work as a Poet," to Dan Mathews for alerting me to the fact that this lecture had been taped, and to Zoe Brown for her faithful transcription. I am also much indebted to Richard Brautigan, Magda Cregg, Norman Davis, Valerie Estes, Joanne Kyger, Gary Snyder and Philip Whalen for valuable assistance.

Grateful acknowledgment is also made to the following for permission to reprint work they first published: The Communication Company, *Evergreen Review*, *O'er*, *The Realist*, *San Francisco Chronicle*, *San Francisco Oracle*.

ESSAYS

MANIFESTO:
BREAD VS. MOZART'S WATCH

I don't think there ever really was a war between the Hip
and the Square, and if there is, I won't fight in it. I am a
Poet. My job is writing poems, reading them out loud,
getting them printed, studying, learning how to become
the kind of man who has something of worth to say. It's
a great job.
Naturally I'm starving to death. Naturally? No, man,
it just does not make sense.
('Look, baby, you want to pay your bills, go out and
get a job.')
I've got a job. I'm a Poet. Why should I do somebody
else's job, too? You want me to be a carpenter? I'm a lousy
carpenter. Does anybody ask a carpenter to write my poems?
But there I am, working 20 hours a day in a salmon
and crab boat (a beautiful job in its own right, but another
story, just as why I didn't make it that way either, is another
story). And suddenly I realize I haven't made a poem in
eight months. Too tired. And I still couldn't pay my bills,
$125 a month in 1962 San Francisco, frugality being one
of the tricks of the Poet Trade.
Meanwhile publishers ('sorry, there's no money for
the Poets') were printing my poems — big Readings got
read (all Benefits, no bread) etc., etc., etc.
So I cracked up. My brain, literally, snapped under
the weirdness of being a Poet, a successful one and being
BECAUSE OF MY JOB (which all agree is noble and good
and all that) an outcast.
PLEASE NOTE: None of this has anything to do with

the Beat Generation, America, Hipness and Squareness —
it's as old as Mozart. I see the basic con as: Bread vs.
Mozart's Watch (don't pay the guy, that would be too
vulgar a return for work so priceless. Give him a watch.
Make sure the watch is engraved with a message that
prevents him from pawning it.)
  So as I say, I cracked up. I took myself to the woods
for almost two years. I sat in a CCC shack 400 miles north
of here, and did my homework. Spring water. Big beautiful
Salmon-River. No bills. Help from home.
  Last November I returned to this city, mostly healed.
Many poems. Some new answers.
  I learned a great many things up there but one of the
strangest is: the plight of the Poet (in fact, the whole
Mozart/Watch con) is partly our fault. THOUSANDS OF
PEOPLE REALLY DO DIG OUR WORTH AND OUR
WORK. THEY REALLY WANT TO HELP — AND THEY
DON'T KNOW HOW!
  If we're so damned Creative, we ought to be able to
solve this problem for our people. And it isn't just a
problem for Poets. It even gets to Ferry Boats. I refuse to
believe a region this rich cannot afford Ferry Boats!
  I stand for Beauty and Delight and Love and Truth
in every form. I am a Poet. I see, finally, that part of my
job is to show how we CAN afford Poetry and Ferry
Boats and good Live Jazz and Dancers and Girls in
Fishbowls — how, in fact, we can't begin to live without
them. Without them the City is only a hideous and
dangerous tough Big Market — of no interest and no
delight and no point to anyone.
  First I have to solve my problem. Without in any
way causing a strain on my community, without
begging or conning anyone in any way, I will pay my
bills entirely by doing my real job, which is Poet.
  Then I can give attention to solving more general

problems — again, without strain, without begging or conning. Charity-Crusade shots are out, for example.

On Friday, June 12th, at 8:30 at the Old Longshoremen's Hall, 150 Golden Gate Street, you can hear some of these discussed in my Poetry — Gary Snyder, Philip Whalen and I will read from our` new work at that time.

See Utopian Visions built before your very eyes! Poems! Delights! As George Herms, local poet/sculptor said: "God says we can, Louise!"

Cheap. $1.

[From Ralph J. Gleason's column "On the Town," *San Francisco Chronicle*, 11 June 1964]

"A MOVING TARGET
IS HARD TO HIT"

Whatever tribe I am the reincarnated member of, apparently
won, or lost, or survived, as Ishi's TRIBE, simply by fading
away, dispersing, a wisp of fog no one can strike: "a moving
target is hard to hit." This can be the reverse of cowardice,
it takes great courage, at times, to back off from what is
rightly your place to stand.

Therefore, this is not advice for all. Some of you are
people who stand there and take it, as the poles did, the ones
who did, attack the hordes of tanks on horseback, with
futile swords. Beautiful, that is your shot. It is not mine.

When 200,000 folks from places like lima ohio and
cleveland and lompoc and visalia and amsterdam and london
and moscow and lodz suddenly descend, as they will, on the
haight-ashbury, the scene will be burnt down. Some will stay
and fight. Some will prefer to leave. My brief remarks are for
those who have a way or ways similar to mine: *disperse.*

Gather into TRIBES of 15 or less. Communal "families"
of 5 adults (however divided into sexes) and the natural
number of children thereby made, is ideal for nomadic
tribal action.

More than 3/4 of the state of california is national
forest, national park, or state forest or park. Take your
truck or car and make your camp in the part of the state
you like most. Most parks require that you move in two
weeks. Some places require moving every two days. This is
only fair. The idea is, no one has the right to hog one campsite for the summer.

Choose unfamous forests. Avoid yosemite. Work,

honestly, with the forest ranger. Write the state of california for their booklet. I think the feds have a similar
campsite guide.

Also, volunteer for summer fire-fighting work. It's
good work, well paid, and necessary. When the fire starts
they come to your camp and take you to the scene of disaster.

Another thing, as I was once quoted: "sometimes you
only have to step 3 feet to the left and the whole insane
machine goes roaring by." Or something like that.

The point is, for those who have this kind of way, not
out of cowardice, but as WAY, that sitting in the haight-
ashbury in all that heat and the terrible crowd you cannot
help anyway (maybe), is simple insanity.

Disperse. Gather into smaller tribes. Use the beautiful
land your state and national governments have already set
up for you, free. If you want to.

Most Indians are nomads. The haight-ashbury is not
where it's at — it's in your head and hands. Take it anywhere.

[Gestetnered by The Communication Company (UPS) 3/27/67]

GREED

The rich man can pass into Heaven about as easily as a
Camel can go through the eye of a needle, and other
images throughout our 4,000-year history of stories by
brave tough-minded men, have it, written down, or
otherwise available.

Christ, before he was old enough to get a drink or
be drafted in America, threw the money-changers out
of the Temple. The story is not clear. Could He have
done so with the Bank of America? And there's a
Walt Whitman Savings and Loan in Walt's home town,
showing us all how famous we'll get if we never cheat.
The rewards are clear, and detestable.

"When did America go wrong?" is a question asked
and asked again, everywhere. Thoreau asked it. Charles
Olson asks it in *The Maximus Poems,* and finds that
fishing, in Gloucester, was out of the hands of fishermen,
and into the hands of usurers (bankers) about 100 years
before our first revolution.

"When did America go wrong" is a question easily
answered. It never was right. And I say this having, deeply,
the dream of what this thing could have been. Could still
be, if people would only get out of our way. Out of
their way.

When I was in grade-school the story was called the
"Triangle Trade." This turns out to be: (1) you buy black
humans from Arabs, in Africa. (2) you sell these people in
Haiti, Jamaica, Cuba, and any other islands in the Gulf.
(3) you get these stolen, black, people to cut the sugar-
cane down, and the cane is rendered into molasses, shipped

8

"up East." turned into Rum, and sold in England.

It turns out to be a triangle of "trading," beginning with stolen black humans and ending with poison, Rum, sold in England.

The whole thing is you have to get it absolutely straight, that "profit motive" means very simply: you give less than you take. If you give less than you take, you grow mean and stingy. Everybody suffers. Morality is totally impossible. "Good guys always lose," said Casey Stengel.

One of my favorites among the many tough, true, things that Kenneth Rexroth has said is this: "People look at our free public library system as something beautifully American, free, liberty, and all that, but the fact is those libraries were built with money that should have been paid to the steel-workers in the first place." (I paraphrase, not having my books handy.)

Greed, then, and Usury (the most pernicious form of greed, the selling of money) have always been the carbuncles on the neck of America. We have never been free.

We are now in the middle of America's third revolution (the second was the Civil War). This one hits America where it lives: "The conscience of most Americans is as thin as the skin of his wallet," said Nelson Algren.

When hundreds of thousands of "scions" they call them, of the greatest fortunes in America refuse to take over Dad's big company, then the revolution will really get going. In 1950 I got the vision that the fun of making huge corportations was over, and the creative thing (as difficult to do right as to build the corporations in the first place), the creative thing is, now, to give the corporations away.

How happy would South America be, if certain

countries were told "United Fruit Company will no longer operate here"! Examples in every corner of this planet are too numerous and too obvious to include here.

Hold only to this one thought: It is now the time for America to give away its corporations. This, and this most of all, is the challenge to intelligence, creativity, or whatever.

Happily, thousands of youngsters understand this. One of the most important aspects of the present revolution, and one I've never seen written up, is the large number of folks, with real big money, who've dropped out.

Here's this kid with outrageous hair, big Harley, and weird leather clothes, in a bar. He looks so young and strange he gets asked for his I.D., produces it, and takes to talking to a friend of mine. This friend of mine is a real Bibliophile, collects and loves books, really, that is, reads them. Memorizes some of them. So, in the course of a long conversation he allows as how his real ambition is to have a perfect bookstore. The kid says, "OK I'll get you one. Tomorrow we'll meet with my lawyer some place. Where?"

And it turned out to be true. There was the lawyer, the kid, the dream, the contract, everything. It's a real good bookstore in Southern California, the "owner" and his "partner" each get about $4,000 a year in salary, the shop makes a small profit which goes toward the investment ($10,000 I'd guess, considering the inventory of books has to be at least $5,000).

What we have here is a young man with money, and enough savvy to underwrite a small business that is needed, and the two whole families get their livings out of it (making it frugally), and the rich kid loses nothing. Maybe gains by tax deductions, etc.

But, and this is so important, think what the rich kid is getting spiritually. We Buddhists insist that temples,

and other offerings, earn us no merit. Well, maybe that is
right in some stern way. But I think this young boy's
offering of this bookstore, and the 2-family faring-well
bit, is meritorious. Of course, it all depends on how he
takes it, or gives it. That's his problem
        But do you know what this kid's damn fool father
did? He, already slated to inherit more money than he
could ever spend, stepped into Daddy's shoes and ran
this huge corporation. Why?
        Let's see it as the true revolution it is. Success, Am-
bition, Yankee Trading, and the rest of that is jazz, just
plain old horseshit jazz. It's clear to those of us who
don't have money, it's clear to those of us who do, and
the removal of Money-as-God from America will crack
America faster than Christ cracked Rome.
        Good riddance.

                        •   •   •   •   •

        "You are all children of the Universe, you have a
right to be here," the anonymous monk said. And while
you are here you must:
                (1)   Eat and drink
                (2)   Sleep
                (3)   Piss and shit
                (4)   Die
(you can conceivably go without balling, though it is not
recommended).
        Since we have to pay money for (buy): (1) our eats
(there being no land not owned, anywhere, anymore) and
(2) a place to sleep or we get arrested, and (3) pay dearly
for the place we shit and piss in, it appears that only a
drink of water is still free, most places. For we certainly
(4) have to pay dearly for death and burial, unless we
are very clever indeed.

We are not free.

We are slaves from the minute of birth until long after death — we're on an eat later, work now, plan (maybe that's what is meant by Original Sin).

In order to pay for these things we cannot live without, we are expected to sell ourselves, not to the Devil (which might be a way better deal), but to a Corporation, a State System of several kinds, a husband, a rich relative, there are a variety of purchasers and the price may vary, but the fact remains we must, in order to live, die a little or a lot.

(Note that we left out breathing, and that the city of Tokyo now has a vending machine which gives you several breaths of good air, and that soon we will all wear metered masks.)

Money is death. Ask yourself why banks and currency use the same images as tombstones.

· · · · ·

But how to do it? And will it happen fast enough? Almost 15 years ago Gary Snyder had the vision: "If nobody bought a new car for just one year, the whole thing would collapse. Then, maybe we could build it right this time."

This country, all countries, get younger every year. By 1970 more than half the population of the world will be under 25.

Some of these will find themselves "owning" huge amounts of money and power. I know one person who, years ago, told me he could "buy" 9 nations — that is, he had more money than these nations had. It nearly drove him mad, did make him a little crazy, because it wasn't his Way to do this thing. He was benign enough, but he didn't want to be a dictator.

Somewhere around $100,000 money stops being

money and turns into power. Thousands of young Americans
have this power. The proper use of it could free the entire
world.
      It will be very difficult. You would have to make
right use of this corporation. You can't just give it away,
because then it falls into greedy hands again. It has to be
put to work, good work, and those who have this power
have to learn what good work is. Not an easy task, but far
simpler than most college profs would have you believe.
Actually, everybody knows what's true and good, it was
there in the first place.
      And perhaps we'll be delivered by the hands of babes.
I sure hope so.

[*San Francisco Oracle,* October 1967]

Poetry is not a diversion.
It can't be called upon to give solace,
however heavy the time.

We, who wish to call the Tribe to dance,
who sing at tribal celebrations, calm the King
(in good times), and then retire

to our mountains, our gardens,
or the hearth,

must always yield to what the secrets of this art decide.

Especially in heavy times, this art decides
there is no thing to do except

perfectly accurate report of
what we thought we saw.

Or put it this way:

If the Tribe refuses to dance,
the Poet can only worry, watch, and
warn.

Therefore: **FINAL CITY / TAP CITY**
             A Crack at the Bottom of It

They grow wherever there is water. From the sea they
mostly look white. Thin concrete skin over bay-shore,
lakeside, riverbank. Big barnacles on the sea rock?
     Dome of foul air, full of radio squeaks, TV signals,
Tadar. Shriek of Jet. Flap flap helicopter. Foulness
flowing into all the very waters that made them come to be.

"Hard, flat, incurable sore, Baltimore."
     Inside, the din is unbelievable.
     Millions of terrified beings scurry through senseless
mazes of tunnels and lanes and doors and corridors. The
senses are insulted. Nose abused. Eyes revolted. Ears unable
to shut it out. Lungs blanketed with lethal dust. Tired feet.
     Everybody rushing about on some little errand some-
body forced him to do. At pain of death. "Faces insane with
purpose." William Burroughs.
     Designed to protect everything inside from everything
outside (*country*, they used to call it). Gradually there was
no "outside."
     Lots of danger, in.

     I
     Cities keep getting bigger and bigger and faster. People,
inside them, get more crazed. Lots of them just can't do it
anymore.
     See him scrubbing that single marble step at the mad-
house. Twenty years and the step is noticeably lower, very
smooth. Or the Veteran, they call him, setting records at
Livermore Hospital for the most wallets ever made in "Leather Therapy." He makes one, and only one, kind of wallet.
Can't get him to go to lunch some days.
     He isn't any crazier than any boss. The main difference
is, he took it all on himself, chose a small part of the world
where he could work, without hurting anybody, and made
that part of the world clean. He's beautiful, at most an inch
away from making it, and miserable, and lost.
     I had a father-in-law, once, a gentle, good, Jewish man
who worked his whole life in City. A newspaper man for
Hearst, in Chicago. He once spent 3 days in a phone booth,
in a race riot. "Nobody wanted to phone, so I was safe
there. And I could phone my stories in." He couldn't always
dart out to piss, even.

He went with us once on a vacation to the Wisconsin
lakes. He was afraid to take a walk in the evenings: "The
deer will put your eyes out with their horns." I tried to
explain my admiration for him, that every corner in Chicago
is far more dangerous, every day.

Unaware of his life of heroism, he trembled in the
forest. But he went out into it, finally. And one fine evening
he was lucky enough to suprise 3 deer only 20 feet away.
They stared at one another for a moment, and when the
deer stately left, he wept at their beauty.

City boy makes good. Age 56.

II

"Temperature Inversion" in London 1962 killed 5,000
folks in 3 days. (Warm air is on top, like a cap, and all the
poisons get trapped in there, inside.)

"Mostly old folks with lung trouble anyway or bad
hearts," they said. Figuring it out, later, they found that
inversion for 5 days, instead of 3, would kill all of London,
man and boy. Ten million London folks done in by the
stink they send to heaven.

Or water. Most cities so vulnerable $50 of TNT in the
right place on the aqueduct and no taps drip. Tap City.
Millions, crazed, killing for a cup of water. Huge profits
from a bathtub.

III

That was no-water. Consider too much of the stuff.

Every summer some parts of Chicago get 3 inches of
rain in 24 hours. No elevators, no lights, no way to get home.

"Wiped out!" they say. "$5,000 for the game room,
not even counting the pool table. Never happened before."

Every summer of the world. Disaster of the 3-inch
rain.

IV

There's a danger too grave even to be named if we stand
on ground we do not know. Most of us stand in City. Few
know what that City is.
     City is not even ground, but thin concrete on top of
ground. Plus human beings, bustling.
     The Planet, as shown by the anecdote of the deer, is
something else. The Planet simply waits there, gentle and
undemanding, until we get out of the way. Leave a city 25
years and grass, trees, berry vines, will crack the sidewalks.
All those hyped-up errands! All those speedy days!

V

It's even worse to stand in meat and skin we do not
know. City destroys our sense of meat and skin, because
City insults every sense we have. Every organ of sense. Every
organ.
     Once I was walking with Phil Whalen at 6th and Mission
and he had to excuse himself. I waited on the corner while
he went into a bar. When he came back he said, "I hate to
piss in skidrow bars, the floors are always wet and I have
holes in my shoes."

VI

There is such a thing as City, and we have to know
what that is. We have to know what ground we're walking
on, or we'll all be suckers and fools. After 25 years with
the Company, a calendar, a hearty handshake, and permission to get through the gate to talk to your friends.
     I always admired Arthur Koestler, and always was
enraged by him. I knew him to be smart, well read, and
almost pathologically honest. Also, he cared a lot about
the things I wanted to know. None of this changed the
fact that I knew Koestler was wrong. "Wrong" is a very
good word. Very few educated people still know how to

use it.

     Just 2 weeks ago I found Koestler giving himself away
to my sense of his wrongness. He says, in *Yogi & the Com-
missar,* that we are a "vulnerable animal, living on a hostile
planet."
     Clearly this man has never looked at his own two hands.
Has never known the miracle of his human eyes. Does not
know he is the only animal which can out-climb a mountain
goat (as the northwest Indians do, chinning themselves on
quarter-inch ledges in the rock, till they drive the goat to
where the goat must fall). Can do that, and also swim. Can
run with the halter in his hand until the horse drops dead.
Can curl up into a ball, as the fox does, let the snow cover
him, for warmth, and make it through a blizzard on Mt.
Shasta. As John Muir did.
     Koestler doesn't know the skin he stands in, the meat
he is, and he doesn't know the ground he's standing on.
What, possibly, can he tell us about anything else?
     All we get are reports from various errand boys (at
pain of death) and very accurate descriptions of organized
insanity.
     Koestler knows he's wrong, he's always cringing about
it. He is the scapegoat, here, not because he's the worst,
but because he's among the best of those who make articulate the European Mind we must (at pain of death) reject.
     Camus and Sartre make the same errors, but have no
humbleness.

          VII

     City is so human. Is it possible that this becomes our
Tragic Flaw? (seeing City as Mindless evolution, irreversible,
Man's way of changing, not biological?)
     Are we doomed to die by City? City for us like Ptero-
dactyl flew his huge, Dinosaur, carcass with his little finger?
Pinky finally 6 feet long and a web of skin for wing, but

everything else was wrong and he cashed in. Victim of super-specialization.

Is it so with us? "The trouble with organization is it's just like perfection, the more you have the more you want." Gertrude Stein.

VIII

No use wading through Sociological swamps how breakdown of family-church-community-morals — "We lost our roots" — causes fidgety kids in the suburb, builds huge head-shrink industry, drives all to dope. Those folks spent all their time trying to figure out *why* it got this way. They never found out, therefore, *where* it had got to. Let alone getting to things to do about it.

Obviously, it's all but over. Even if you don't, as I haven't yet, bring in the Big Bomb.

And what this realization has done is to create a huge number of people who are Immigrants in their own native land. This may be almost the first time it's happened. Always, before, there was somewhere to go. Even Moses could march his folks away.

But this is the full circle. Uruburus has taken his tail in his mouth. Man has always moved westerly, now is piling up on the Pacific Cliffs, and Japan is flooding back on us. It is all One. At last.

IX

It's hard to say what to do about it, because it may be too late, and what small things are being done about it are just now starting. Or say it: It may be all over already, and it isn't even started yet.

The "Total Assault on the Culture" by Ed Sanders, and Diggers, and all who identify with the Hip, will certainly produce a whelm of beautiful souls, it already has. Whether it will save the species is a very grave, and doubtful, question.

Immigrants on their own native soil have already estab-
lished a style which has much to commend it. We have
kicked the habits of Success, Ambition, Cleanliness/God-
liness, Duty, Purpose, Loyalty, Citizenship, and in some
rare and truly beautiful instances, as with Allen Ginsberg,
the loss of European sense of "Self."

Like all Immigrants, we band together to save energy.
Jews, coming to New York, banded together in sixes and
nines and bought a Brownstone house, for cash. They ate
together at a common table. Freed of rent and eating well
and easy (you can feed 12 or more people for the same
price as 3), they could turn their pushcarts into million-
dollar estates.

Today their children get high together. Work little,
eat well, ball like crazy, and use all their energy to perfect
their own beings, and to help the perfection of others.

It may be an ugly word in America, but this is a re-
ligious revolution, just like the first one, and less hung up.
Like, everybody fucks.

The worst Persian voluptuary could not have dreamed
our most ordinary day.

X

Gluttony, greed, lack of compassion, has caused America to become the most despised nation on Earth. The sad
thing is, my Polish Lady tells me, we were throughout her
youth, and still are, or could be, the hope of all.

We face great holocausts, terrible catastrophies, all
American cities burned from within, and without.

However, our beautiful Planet will germinate — underneath this thin skin of City, Green will come on to crack
our sidewalks! Stinking air will blow away at last! The bays
flow clean!

And there will be signs. We will know when to slip
away and let these murderous fools rip themselves to pieces.

In the meantime, stay healthy. There are hundreds of miles to walk, and lots of work to be done. Keep your mind. We will need it. Stake out a retreat. Learn berries and nuts and fruit and small animals and all the plants. Learn water. For there must be good men and women in the mountains, on the beaches, in all the neglected and beautiful places, so that one day we come back to ghostly cities and try to set them right.

There must not be a plan. We have always been defeated by our Plan.

In all that rubble, think of the beautiful trinkets we wave about our heads as we dance!

As we do right now. As we do *right* now.

[*The Realist*, "The Digger Papers," August 1968]

BRAUTIGAN'S MOTH
BALANCED ON AN APPLE

Those who'd read Richard Brautigan's *Trout Fishing in America* will be pleased to know that his new book, *In Watermelon Sugar*, is written even better than that, and is even more beautiful.

Nobody understands where Brautigan got his way of putting words together. I suppose you have to call it prose — there they are, little blocks of paragraphs that go from margin to margin on the page. And I suppose you have to call *In Watermelon Sugar* a novel — it has chapters and a plot, people fall in and out of love, there is even gore and violence in it. But there is nothing like Richard Brautigan anywhere.

Perhaps, when we are very old, people will write "Brautigans," just as we now write novels. Let us hope so. For this man has invented a genre, a whole new shot, a thing needed, delightful, and right. At the same time, and this is very important, Brautigan's style, strange as it is, is as easy to read as the plainest prose of say, science fiction or detective stories. You start in, and within three pages you are trapped until the book ends.

In Watermelon Sugar is mainly a landscape, a place of Mind, gentle, haunting, and beautiful. There is something called iDeath, a small village or living room or something, surrounded by the Forgotten Works, a sort of super-dump of Mind. Ordinary people wander about doing their deeds with a gentleness and grace as precarious as a "moth balancing on an apple." That last quote is from the book. But there is something very ominous about *In Watermelon Sugar*.

It's as devastating as *End Game* for the same reasons,

even though it gets there from an entirely different direction. In *End Game* Beckett arrives at his vision through images of unrelenting despair and ugliness. *In Watermelon Sugar* moves through images of relentless poignancy and beauty. It is almost too beautiful, too simple, tender and sweet. Like watermelon sugar itself. But he pulls it off, and drags us into a world of love and peace and simple reward. A place where we could eat, talk, make perfect love, with a minimum of bother to ourselves and all the world.

What gets you in the gut is we're probably not good enough for that, it would drive us crazy, and besides the Forgotten Works are looming there, all around us, and it would be so easy. It would be so easy. And it won't happen. Except a few of us are doing it right now. And it never was. Except it went that way for those with the heart to do it. All through time. In every Place.

It's the same old end game, but Richard chooses to go down with nothing less than the most beautiful girls, meals, daily deeds, and long night walks, looking at our total Loss. Yours and mine. If we let it.

To get the point fully, you have to know how Richard is. Not who he is, that would be impossible to write. Even Richard may never be able to do that.

Richard Brautigan is now 33 years old. In the days of the Beat Generation he was a precocious guy — 20 years old when everybody else was 29. He wrote a lot of poetry, fathered girls* and tried to raise them. He succeeded. They are still alive and living somewhere else. He didn't dump them. They, and their mother, just went away.

Every book of Richard's has a picture of a different and more beautiful chick on the cover. It's his trademark. The sign of a man who is often lonely, but seldom alone.

One of the youngest members of the Beat Generation,

* Richard Brautigan tells me he has fathered but one daughter. Ed.

he is one of the oldest members of the Hippy Thing — the Haight Ashbury slide of it all. He is a Digger. One of the people who fed the mob on that now sad street. Many of his poems were free poems, poems printed by the Communications Co. and given away, free. On the street.

This man is a real writer, an inventor of Form, Man of the street, and first-rate human being.

[*San Francisco Chronicle*, 15 December 1968]

PHILIP WHALEN AS
YELLOWSTONE NATIONAL PARK

This is an important book. Until now, the poetry of Philip
Whalen could be found only in Little Magazines or in editions
so small they quickly sold out. *On Bear's Head* is a collection
of nearly all his work, more than twenty years of it, in one
volume. One of this century's most brilliant poets is at last
accessible to all.
 Whalen's poetry is not difficult. Great poetry never is.
Anybody can understand exactly what is being said, though
it may take several readings to appreciate how deeply considered his "meanings" are. The poems are wise, not smart.
They aren't grim. He reaches us, mostly, through wit and a
cranky insistence upon joy. Most important, he makes poetry
of the actual language of the street.
 In 1956, when I was an advertising writer in Chicago,
people kept asking me "what kind of poetry is this 'beat'
thing we keep hearing about?" I mimeographed the following Whalen poem (which I had from a letter he sent me) and
I passed it around.

    FURTHER NOTICE

 I can't live in this world
 And I refuse to kill myself
 Or let you kill me.

 The dill plant lives, the airplane
 My alarm clock, this ink
 I won't go away

25

I shall be myself —
Free, a genius, an embarrassment
Like the Indian, the buffalo

Like Yellowstone National Park.

Soon, "Yellowstone National Park" was used by secretaries, bosses, whatever kind of wage slave, as a way of showing their integrity when things got tough. These poems are useful.
They are also brilliant and swift. One of my favorites ["Hymnus Ad Patrem Sinensis"] goes:

I praise those ancient Chinamen
Who left me a few words,
Usually a pointless joke or a silly question
A line of poetry drunkenly scrawled on the margin of
    a quick splashed picture — bug, leaf,
    caricature of Teacher
on paper held together now by little more than ink
& their own strength brushed momentarily over it

Their world & several others since
Gone to hell in a handbasket, they knew it —
Cheered as it whizzed by —
& conked out among the busted spring rain cherryblossom
    winejars
Happy to have saved us all.

That's a lot of ground to cover in a breath, and he makes it swing, hard as jazz, straight as talk. It's the new America speaking. Away old Puritan greed! Marx? Forget it. Freud? Goodbye! Hello crazy old-time China.
And the Zen Mind Whalen respects and uses is given back to us in American speech and imagery. He "makes it new" out of his Oregon Mind. His Bear's Head. He does this

knowing he is doing it. It is not a case of untrained magic
genius. Whalen is that rare scholar who is in it only because
he wants to know. Some books he prefers to challenge with
a poem. Others, he venerates. Not since Rexroth, and before
him Pound, have we had in America a man who respects, and
knows, his forefathers so well.

He loves music, all of it. He plays at Bach, badly, on
tinny, borrowed, pianos. Once, after four hours of "tinkle-
tinkle," stop, tinkle, "damn," he said, "There is not a single
piece of piano music I can play all the way through without
making a mistake." Then off to Ornette Coleman, or elec-
tronic sounds of Subotnick, John Cage, Ives, anything. Certainly this accounts for the great range of his meters. I don't
know of any poet this century who has broken more new
ground, formally, than Whalen. He can make anything work,
whereas most poets, e. e. cummings comes to mind, find a
music and stick pretty close to it all their lives. This is
another reason why, although Whalen is not so famous as
the more dramatic members of his generation, the poets
themselves pretty well agree that he has few peers.

Some of our more conservative readers and writers of
poetry maintain he's only silly and flippant. Apparently
they want to believe that it's got to be painful and dull or it
can't be deep. Gloom. What a shame these people have missed
the hundreds of years of laughter and teachings of Zen Luna-
tics, Idiot Savants, DaDa (which so frightened our grand-
parents and so quickly cleaned things up). Yes, there is an
almost arrogant "why not?" in Whalen, as there was in
Charles Parker, as there is in all the arts today. We are breaking loose. The feeling is one of joy and relief. And laughter,
zany wit, can cut through so much grease, so fast. Whalen is
a master of this part of it, too.

There is only one bad thing about the book. For $17.50
we expect, and get, exquisite books, printed on fine paper,
with stiff boards bound in raw silk, and maybe a picture or

two, in color. This is a plain, trade, edition — the kind of
book we now pay, maybe, $8.50 for. There isn't even an
alphabetical index of titles and first lines, and the book has
326 poems in it. The price is outrageous. Is this an attempt
to set some ugly precedent?

What really hurts is Whalen walks with that stubborn
army of penniless poet-scholars who will suffer great priva-
tions if that be necessary to get the work done. He has
averaged less than $17.50 a week for twenty years. Whalen
is an heroic symbol of frugality even in the dropout scene
— a serious man whose simple and richly productive life
has taught us all a most important lesson. To abuse such a
stance this way is scandalous.

[*San Francisco Chronicle*, 22 June 1969]

LANGUAGE IS SPEECH

Preface

Since 1965 I have been teaching a class for the University of California Extension called Poetry Workshop 819. There is no credit for the course and it is open to all. This year, 1970, my course was dropped for budgetary reasons, and I miss teaching it so badly I decided to write a written form of the course. I say "write a written form of the course" because the course itself could never be transcribed since its nature is oral and dependent upon the kind of students who happen to take it.

I always try to have a working writer as a guest for at least one meeting (we used to meet ten Tuesday nights for two hours) and once Allen Ginsberg was the one. I barked for one hour (Allen surprised and delighted me by dropping in unannounced so I just kept on going with whatever I was talking about) and after the break Allen gave a beautiful talk about and demonstration of chanting.

After the class, over drinks, I told Allen I had become a little concerned about the form of the class, that gradually over the five years it had distilled into a loose, rambling, skip-about thing that was really a course in Lew Welch, 1A. "Of course," he said, "all they want is to see and hear a live poet. Where else can they find one?"

•

That is one way of going at it. Another way is to think of what language is from the long historical building of it.

In America we speak and write American English, which

is completely different from British English, and it all comes from the Sanskrit, we are told, but we learned it from our parents and our friends. It is all we have. Our native speech.

Of course there are other speeches we have, from reading. We have Walpole saying: "I write to relieve, not the emptiness of my purse, but the fullness of my mind." It is almost impossible to read that sentence aloud without going into a British accent.

American English has sentences in it like Burroughs': "Motel, motel, motel loneliness blows across the continent like foghorns blowing over still oily tidal water rivers."

•

And to know how recent it is! Whitman had no language to write in. There was no American English when he wrote, which is why his poetry seems so awkward at times. For all his rightness and greatness we have to see Whitman as a man fumbling among languages, the British, the French and the emerging American.

•

Language is speech. You ought to be able to say language is speech and then get on with the rest of it, but you can't because so very few believe it.

Language is what goes on when you open the door of a banquet-room and there are 300 ladies having lunch. It is very interesting to hear. It rises and falls, and every once in an inexplicable while it will suddenly stop, there will be a total silence, and then all 300 ladies will hear that silence and comment on it at the same moment. Then you get a roar.

Language is speech. Any other form, the printed one or the taped one, is a translation of language. All poems

are translations. This book is a translation of the speech I
use when I teach this course, talking to people.
   Once I lived in an upstairs room with a single window
in it. Outside the window was a large date palm tree. Every
sparrow for miles around slept in that palm tree. The din
each evening was unbelievable, and it was the same thing
every dawn, hundreds of sparrows chattering to each other
about where they were to sleep and how it went last night
or whatever.
   That is language. Speech. The din of a Tribe doing its
business. You can't control it, you can't correct it, you can
only listen to it and use it as it is.
   If you want to write you have to want to build things
out of language and in order to do that you have to know,
really know in your ear and in your tongue and, later, on
the page, that language is speech. But the hard thing is that
writing is not talking, so what you have to learn to do is to
write as if you were talking, and to do it knowing perfectly
well you are not talking, you are writing.

Chapter One

You ought to be able to say "language is speech" and then
get on with it, but you can't because so very few people
believe it. And if you believe that language is anything other
than speech you can't even begin to start knowing what
reading and writing is all about.

No one would ever argue that Bach's *music* is the collection of little black notes on paper, but nearly everybody
thinks language has something to do with libraries and dictionaries, and that you can "learn" it through the study of
good books and grammar. Dictionaries, James Sledd used
to say, are the record of usage of people about two generations ago. The street writes dictionaries, the able lexogra-
pher is a recorder and statistician with a fine ear for the
language, the speech, of a tribe.

Whatever is written down is a translation of a speech.
It cannot become language until it is "played," respoken.

I never used the word "respoken" before. Isn't it nice?

You have to love language to be a reader and a writer,
have to have language in a way different from ordinary
speakers. You have to have language in a concrete way
where the words and the structures are held, not simply as
ways to get a thing said, but as a cabinetmaker holds his
tools and his wood.

It takes a gift of ear as definitely as music does. You
can train the ear, make yourself able to hear yourself hearing without losing what is being said, but if you're born
speech-deaf you're as irreclaimable as a tone-deaf musician.

Another analogy with music comes to mind. A student
at the freshman level of a fine music school had perfect
pitch, but was so meter-dumb he couldn't march with the
football band even though he was right next to the bass

32

drum. His "music" was very strange. It existed outside of
time. He won all kinds of prizes as a kid in some small town
but couldn't play *with* anybody else.

Some people are meter-dumb with language. They cannot
hear or produce a structure. The words sort of roll along one
after the other and miraculously refuse to make any kind of
pattern. A good writer should have a good enough ear to hear
this phenomenon well enough to transcribe it. Thomas Mann's
Peppercorn. An amazing feat, to hear and handle non-structure.

We'll get into that later, with Gertrude Stein.

And we must digress here in deference to John Cage
and Ives. Let's go back to the tone-deaf man and music.

Ives' father was the choirmaster of a small church and
led the congregation in the hymns. One of the members was
a huge Swede who just loved to sing, who sang very loud,
and who never hit one note "right." Other members com-
plained to Mr. Ives, couldn't he somehow make the man be
quiet because he was throwing everybody else off? Ives said,
"Have you ever looked at that man's eyes when he's singing?
Have you ever listened to what he *does*? That man knows
more about music than any of you."

Which brings up another fascinating thing. You can
have a fine ear, but you can't, maybe, get the note into
your throat as the ear hears it. My wife is this way. Magda
can hear as well or better than I can, proves this by being
able to tune instruments and hi-fi sets better than most
people. But she can't "carry a tune." It's very strange to
hear her singing in the bathtub. It's like the big Swede: it's
all "wrong" but it is *music* far more beautiful and true than
all the Judy Garlands and Barbra Striesands in the world.

Some people have a very fine ear for the words of
others, but have difficulty bringing their own words to Mind.
"Bringing your words to Mind" is the whole thing, too.
We'll gradually get to that.

Right now I want to get into an imitation of two hours

speaking-time as much as possible about language and speech and the ear and different ways we can all go about it.

One of my most beneficial teachers was James R. Sledd, the distinguished structural linguist at the University of Chicago. At Reed College I did my thesis on Gertrude Stein, and that study convinced me that if I were ever to learn about writing I'd have to stop reading and start looking flat at the stuff of writing itself. So I took history of English and structural linguistic courses from Sledd.

The man really altered my mind — really showed me the wonders and mysteries of this thing we call language. First of all, he forever removed my prejudices regarding dialect.

Like my wife, Sledd had a wonderful ear but could not, even slightly, mimic any dialect other than his own. He spoke in the broadest, flattest, Georgia-cracker accent imaginable. I was shocked. I was raised in California where you're taught to believe that Oakies are inferior, and here I was in graduate school taking linguistics, and Chaucer's English yet, from a Cracker!

Sledd got right into it. "You are probable struck by the way I talk, so let's get it straight right now. I can't mimic. I was always a bright kid and I got a scholarship to Harvard and there I learned you shouldn't say runnin' and jumpin' and kickin', you should say runnING and jumpING and kickING." (And he was a riot saying those words, the "G" sound struck like the natives of Long Island say "Lon Guyland.") "Well, " he went on, "one day I came home and smelled this wonderful smell and I said to my wife, *Honey, are we having fried chickING tonight?*, and then I said to myself, *Sledd, you are a fraud.*"

He then gave a marvelously witty lecture about how he had a good ear but couldn't mimic any other dialect and how it had nothing of importance to do with language other than to indicate how the man's mother and father talked, and how at the end of the course we could hear him try to read Chaucer, a treat.

Language is speech, but speech is not dialect. You can read Faulkner without imitating his Mississippi dialect and you'll lose nothing. Dialect is only a regional and personal voice-print. This is very difficult for many people to believe, but it is so. You can easily separate structure and meaning from dialect, and still be dealing with sound, with the music, with speech, with another's Mind.

Gertrude Stein perfectly mimicked the rhythms and structures of the speech of Baltimore Blacks in her story *Melanctha,* and she didn't transcribe the dialect at all — that is, didn't have to misspell a lot of words to get the work done. Nelson Algren has many many passages with no misspellings, but he catches the real flow of a regional speech.

It took poor Sledd nearly six weeks to rid me of my terrible prejudice. One day I finally heard what the man was doing with language. I heard, really heard, the beautiful structures he made as he talked. He could extemporize a sentence with 20, 30, or even 50 clauses in it and the clarity was blinding.

He freed me also of my stupid idea that there was a right and wrong grammar. There is only grammar. Grammar is the word we use to mean the description of the structure of speech. Period. And we all know our grammar perfectly, otherwise we couldn't be understood. Grammar is the description of the structure of something that's already made, and we know the meaning of an utterance because of the structure, not because of the word-meanings only.

Sledd's example, one of them, was this. Suppose you found a telegram on a man's desk and you don't know the man or anything about him. The telegram reads: *Ship Sails Today.* There is no way to know whether the telegram refers to a ship sailing today, or is a request to ship some sails to some yachtsman. You can't know, because the structure is not given. You make the structure by putting in the *the.*

Ship *the* Sails Today, *The* Ship Sails Today.

There are lots of long books about all this and 1A is
not a linguistics course, so I don't want to get bogged down
here. But here is an example of my own invention which
gets us into the neighborhood of what we're saying.

I once was a bus-driver for a private grammar school
in Chicago. One of my favorite kids was a boy named Mark
in about the 4th grade. I asked him how he was doing and
he said he was having a lot of trouble writing because he
didn't know what a sentence was.

"I don't know what a sentence is is a sentence." I said.
"Is it?"
"Is it is a sentence."
"It is?"
"It is is a sentence, and so is it is is a sentence."

And so on, playing the game all afternoon. Finally I
asked him to say something that was not a sentence. He
couldn't do it. "I can't," he said. "I can't is a sentence" said
I, and then I told him to put a capital at the beginning of
one of those things and a period at the end of it, and to pre-
tend he was talking when he wrote — to talk it first, and
then write it down.

Then I said, "You told me a story about your grand-
mother the other day, let's write it down." He did, and from
that paper forward was always the best writer in his class.

This part of it is so simple only true readers and writers
and language-lovers can understand it. It is all ear, it is all
already understood, it is all totally mysterious.

Language is as much a part of having Human being as
anybody's left leg or liver. It's totally organic. You can't
change it, correct it, or get along without using it. When
Trappists and others take vows of silence they are really
taking on something. The spiritual intensity which results
must be terrifying, and my guess is few non-speakers do
more than withdraw. Try it, for even a day or two.

In the Zen Koan: You are bound hand and foot and
are hanging by your teeth from the branch of a tree which
is leaning out over the void. Rats are nibbling at the roots
of the tree. Somebody comes by and says *What is Zen?* You
must speak. What do you say?

Must speak always struck me as meaning *being human,*
you must.

Once Whalen ended a letter with: *I speak as clearly as*
possible considering that my mouth is full.

•

I don't know the answer to that Koan but I do see this
thing we call language as an inexhaustible delight and wonder.
It constantly comes out of the mouths of the people, a vast
din which will not stop. Its origin is lost. Its changes are
unexplainable. Its structures are indescribable.

Somewhere about two or three years old we begin talking in what is called a sentence. No linguist has been able to
come up with a general description of what a sentence is.
Yet everybody knows what it is, as we saw in the case of
Mark.

There is a beautiful set of books by Jespersen which
begins with the sentence *Birds fly* and which keeps at it for
several volumes until you get to things like *In Italy where*
the thermal currents are such that swallows and other cliff-
dwelling denizens are unable to maintain purchase, the birds,
while seeking shelter and food, fly no less rapidly than their
English counterparts. (I just made that one up now in haste,
Jespersen's building is far more interesting.) And when he
was through he had gotten nowhere near an adequate description or analysis of the English sentence.

Anyone could get a Ph. D. thesis, at once, if he could
do this — be the paper less than one page long.

Add to this mystery the inexplicable changes you can

trace through even a cursory study of the history of English
or any other language, and you do see language as a huge
growth handy for our use but forever beyond our ken.

Nobody knows why the great vowel shift occurred in
English. Nobody knows why love used to rhyme with prove
but no longer does. Nobody knows why the distinction between shall and will is no longer important to us. And the
subjunctive is definitely disappearing as many of the old
do forms did.

It is enough to know *that* these things happened and
are happening and always will go on happening. We humbly
listen to the din of the Tribe and balance ourselves on the
edge of it, like a surfer on a huge wave.

Sledd used to get letters from the public like *My son
can't seem to learn the proper way to use who and whom.*
He answered *Tell your son never to use whom in conversation.* He pointed out to us that when you answer a telephone
To whom am I speaking you are now saying two things, you
are saying *I don't know who is on the other end of this line*
and you are also saying *I am a pedant.* If you want to make
it known that you are a pedant fine, but if not, not. And
there is no way to get out of this bind. Language is final.
What is said is said. Whether you like it or not.

•

Intellectually much of the foregoing is baby talk, somewhere around A, B, and C, in the alphabet of Mind. Don't
be surprised or ashamed if the simpleness of the clump of
observations is hard to believe. I had the very best teachers,
was born glib and gifted with an ear for language, and it was
years before these things became obvious and delightful,
available to ear and speech.

My years of teaching, reading the works of students,
their poems and papers, convinces me that starting with this

quick *language is speech* business is necessary and helpful.

You can't go wrong with these arguments. At worst you can get your ear to working, and at best you can throw out all those tortured sentences you used to call a poem.

•

Based upon all this, but much more interesting, is the whole question of how words come to Mind.

Whatever it is inside there it is certainly, in the beginning, not words. It can come to be words, probably will if the need is real enough, as organically as the steady juicing of the glands, but first of all it is not yet words. How do we bring words to Mind?

I am sitting at my typewriter now bringing out these words to get them off my Mind. I am trying to transmit something, in words. They come out faster or slower and make a pattern, actually many patterns, and it all goes back and forth.

Whalen once said: *The problem is how to get out of my way.*

There are also the problems of whether I am remembering or thinking or making or talking or writing.

•

Once, on the way to Oregon, I stopped at a California winery to get free wine from the tasting room. Just at that time a tour was starting so I decided to go along. A young man of about 23 was the guide and began that strange kind of language guides use, almost a chant: . . . *and on the left a 1500 gallon redwood barrel containing Burgundy kept always at the temperature of . . .* and then he said *Whose kid is that?*

The force of *whose kid is that* caused everyone to pay

attention to the real moment we were all in. A small child was about to fall into a very deep vat of wine.

I vowed, at that moment, that every statement in my poems should have at least the force of *whose kid is that.*

It is an impossible standard, but a good one. Few really bad lines can stand against it.

The guide was chanting remembered lines to a vapid audience. The distance between his Mind, our Minds, and the subject of wine-making simply was not being bridged. But the endangered child called words to his Mind which were immediate and un-premeditated — it was organic, as a leap would be if one were frightened by a truck.

•

In "What Are Master-pieces and Why Are There So Few of Them" Gertrude Stein points out that writing deals constantly with the problem of the difference between thinking and remembering. Writing must never be remembering. If it is, it is a confusing bore. But, as Stein points out, thinking and remembering are so nearly the same thing.

Everyone knows the difference between thinking and remembering, some more keenly than others, but all of us really do know that there is a difference. Perhaps the story of the guide in the winery helps.

The guide in the winery, at the moment he said *Whose kid is that*, was using language in an exact relationship with his consciousness. He was trying to get some work done. He spoke without thinking or remembering. He simply spoke. And the people on the tour responded immediately, without thought. The child, thereby, was saved.

Poetry should be at least as intense as this. It very seldom is.

The few poems we prize over the centuries and across all cultures and times are *more* intense than this.

•

How do we bring words to Mind?

The answer is we bring words to Mind in all sorts of ways for all sorts of purposes and in every degree of intensity and accuracy. Some few bringing of words to Mind we call poems.

How are the words of a poem brought to Mind?

•

When I was Chief Copy Editor of Montgomery Ward and Co. my job was to check the ads the 45 copywriters under me wrote. They were very simple-minded word structures. *This is a refrigerator. It is big and white. Every time you open the door the light turns on. It keeps things cold. Wards sells refrigerators for less than most folks. Buy now. Save.*

This and similar messages had to be bent into interesting patterns, or at least space-filling patterns, over and over again, about all of the familiar items we have in our homes. There should be information: how big is it? why is it more expensive than the other models? what reason is there to buy it now instead of later?

Even at this mundane a level the art of writing proved so demanding to the copywriters (and many of them were gifted; Sherwood Anderson had precisely this kind of job) that there was a joke among the other employees about the *copywriter's trance.*

It was true. You could go through the seas of desks and spot a working copywriter every time. He or she would be staring straight ahead, perhaps with a half-smile but mostly with a vacant sort of puzzled frown, and then *peck peck peck* on the typewriter, and then another frozen, vacant, trance-like staring at nothing. Then *peck peck peck* again. Occasionally a furious burst.

The trance was respected by the other employees. You waited until the concentration broke, and only then did you ask whatever question you had in mind.

•

The copywriter in his trance is neither thinking nor remembering, though his mind is doing things that partake of both. He is writing. He is bringing words to Mind. He is doing this in an unusual way, that is to say he is doing it in a way we don't ordinarily see him do it in conversation, or while buying cabbages in the market or making change.

He is bringing words to Mind in writing rather than in talking. It is an important difference. It is almost impossible for him to say *Whose kid is that* with the absolute directness of the winery guide. But this directness, or the semblance of it, should, I think, always be his goal.

•

He is in a trance. And all he is trying to do is make his living writing baby-talk ads for a mail-order house.

But Li Po, while extemporizing intricate lines on whatever subject the Emperor happened to throw at him, dropped, I am sure, into the same glazed-eyed state. His eyes would then clear, and he'd wittily speak his lines.

I saw William Carlos Williams do this on a challenge from Snyder and Whalen and me in 1950.

There is clearly something special about the way we bring words to Mind when we write. We do something different from what we do even when we exactly speak, as the winery guide exactly spoke and saved the child. (Usually, of course, we don't speak with any exactness at all. It is mostly ceremony and blather.)

With any exactness? Exactness to what?

•

What we try to do in the situation of teaching or writing or confessing or standing firm against those who would cheat us or lie to us or kill us, what we try to do when we need most to speak openly to our beloved or to those who believe in us, need us, ask us for really necessary advice, is to try to be, in words, exact. We must now speak. And we must now be exact. To what?

This is the moment you bring words to Mind as the poet brings words to Mind. It is why we prize poetry, in spite of all the sloppy examples of writing that go under the name of poetry. We all know what we go to poetry for. We want the exact transmission of Mind into Word.

•

We don't care how crazy that man is, we want exact transmission of that crazed Mind. We are crazed ourselves. It would help to know we are not alone. We are delighted by the calmness of this other one. We are sent to the woods to see, really see, what we'd so often looked at and never noticed at all, by that other Mind. We need to know exactly what it must be like to be an ambassador, a killer, a hulking fool.

•

Since the business of living has so many barbs in it, and since so many of our friends are liars or fools or inarticulate or emotionally blunt or are sucking on us for what they imagine we can give though we can't, it is pure joy to read the poems of the truth-sayers, the simple singers, the masters of prayer and devotion, and the crazed, wise, babblers of Ecstacy, the High-Mind Singers to no end.

Exactness? Exactness to what? You know what you
want in the writing you read, and you know how seldom you
get it. We want exact transmission of Mind, in words (we
can get it in dance, occasionally, or music, just as seldom,
in painting just as now and then, but in this book we are
thinking about writing and reading and so we are talking
about words, and how they come to Mind).

.

The words come to Mind through the whole history of
whatever Tribe you learned your language in. The words come
to Mind through all the private history of how you've lived
your Human Being. There is no way to cheat, unless you go
to too many schools, and try to be a poet.
Try to be a poet? What a blasphemy!
Unless you mean, as Gregory Corso did when he got
the calling in a prison in New York, to use the native speech
which is as much a part of you as your eyes and hair, and
mean to use it to the end of truth and life (against all odds
in a deranged world), to use this speech, your own speech,
the language of your father and your mother and your
friends, the primary tool of all your actions toward all your
wants and needs, to use this speech as a weapon, a tool, a
singer's voice, the means to total sharing of all your Mind,
unless you mean to do that, then to try to be a poet is a
blasphemy.

.

Accuracy. Accuracy to what? Exactness. Exactness to
what?
Maybe we ought to say the words *are brought* to Mind,
because the more you work with this process the more it
seems, as the Muse Idea has it, that the words *come* to Mind,

unasked.

I was taking a nap in the afternoon of a hot day in Chicago. I had a dream in which I was reading a very long book, 1500 pages, called *Expediencyitis*. I dreamt it was written by a German, name blurred. The form of the book was the form of this one: blocks of paragraphs divided by centered dots. I was struck, in my dream, by the great wisdom of the book, and eagerly read page after page.

I began to awake.

As I began to awake I had several thoughts. I was sorry the dream was going to come to an end because the book I was reading was so very wise and beautiful. Then I had the thought, while still dreaming, that of course if I was the dreamer then I had written the book, not the blurry German. It was my book. It was what I, if I could only write better, would write. (I was about 26 years old with very few real poems.)

I then dreamed (thought/dreamed) that I'd surely not be able to remember and write down any of those beautiful and profound paragraphs. I was almost awake.

I then thought/dreamed the idea of going back into the dream and capturing some of the text of *Expediencyitis* with the idea of writing it down if I could find some of it. I was successful. I went back into the dream and came back with a single piece from the book.

> Through the years of her speech
> a persistent gong
> told us how grief had
> cracked the bell of her soul.

I wrote this down while still drowsy, and it was three months before I realized that this was a poem about my mother. *Us* is my sister and I, and my mother really had, through the years of her speech, told us of her grief. The

gong, told, bell (with *cracked* working in there as in the
Liberty Bell) are pieces of craft (craft?) totally unavailable
to me at the time of this dream, and rarely available to me
now.
　　Imagine what the rest of that book said.

                                          •

　　Accuracy. Exactness.
　　We have to be exactly accurate to what we have in Mind.
That is all we have.
　　If we are to make of that Mind in words, then we have
to be absolutely accurate in the way we use our native
speech, since that, too, is all we have. It is our only language.
　　The shape of our Mind is the shape of our native speech,
since our native speech helped to shape our Mind.
　　"Mind is shapely." Mind speaks in many ways.

                                          •

　　"Mind is shapely." Mind speaks in many ways.
　　Perhaps you are a dancer. Others, as John Cage did,
show Mind in the form of music. Finally, John Cage has
become a writer, a very accurate and exact one, a true poet
of American language, a heavy case in favor of my argument
about ear-training.
　　Or maybe, as my friend Jack Boyce is, you are a painter.
He is truly a painter. He is astonished that I can't see things
in his paintings which are obvious to him, since I dearly love
paintings and know a great deal about looking at them. I am
occasionally surprised by his inability to see some nice (nice
means precise, but has been misused) thing in a piece of writing. He is a painter, I am a poet.
　　There are many ways to bring the Thing to Mind.
　　Now I said the shape of our Mind is the shape of our

native speech, since our native speech helped to shape our Mind. But in a more general way we have to realize that I am a word man, that I have *speech* in my vocabulary with a peculiarly heavy emphasis.

Actually the whole thing about the different arts is that they all do the same thing in any place and at any time though they do use different materials.

The reason they do the same thing at any particular place and time, depending on the alertness of a particular art-form as compared to some other one, is that the Mind of a time and place must be One. Mind is always One, but it is always easier to see how that is if you look at a particular place and time. You see how shapely it is.

Our time is just as shapely as any of the others, the 18th Century or the Tang Dynasty or whatever you may choose to see as one-of-a-piece. When you live in a time, as we all must do, it is hard to see it as anything except discordant.

But our time is going along with perfect order, we are all of one Mind, it only is hard to prove it and of course there are a large number of people alive now and in power who are of the Mind of two generations ago. This is always so. Perhaps now it is more dangerous than in previous periods, but the fact is power has always been in the hands of those who live as if the world were what it was two generations before.

Gertrude Stein made the distinction between those who live *in* their generation and those who are *of* their generation. Those *in* their generation are always thinking two generations back, those *of* their generation are *making* the thing as it really is being made. Of course it is not there yet.

It is really an exhilarating thing to be *of* your generation, and especially lately it is scary and important to know that now I am 44 years old and frequently I find myself holding on to something back there in the Beat Generation

days and the thing has slid by me, like an ocean wave. There
is no saving it. It is over. It is going to be something. It is
good to feel yourself as one who helps it along, whatever
it may be. And to notice how it is, not as it ought to be,
but how it really is. And can you ride it? Can you sing it?
Will it, and this is presently a real concern, get too heady
for you to handle? The safe ways are now, at 44, becoming
far too available.

•

    We are still talking about Language as Speech and how
that has to do with writing and reading. We got into Mind
unavoidably, since after all you do bring the words up out
of your Mind, there being no other source. And we became
interested in the question of how you do that, how you
get what is not words into words (or dance or paint or
sculpture or whatever it is you do to make Mind something
out there for the others to use, though you have the perfect
right to just let it buzz in there for your own joy entirely).
    But that never is enough. We are makers. Those of us
who are fortunate enough to be able to handle the daily
living business and still find time to learn ornate crafts become what the world calls artists. Some of us go straight to
being artists without learning how to handle the simple daily
tasks. But the happiest men and women in the world are
those of us who find that if we don't, actively, make the
chores of the day too difficult, there'll be lots of time left
for the play we call art. And that if we do that we have the
added joy of friends and strangers who love to see or hear
or feel what we do, and we have the even greater pleasure
of being able to meet, as peers, the other maniacs who live
the way we live, and make the way we make. If it were still
possible to be a romantic, I would say I have lived my life
as if I thought I were a hero, and I know for a fact that all

of my dearest friends are heroes and heroines to their toes.
    The worst Persian voluptuary could not have dreamed
my most ordinary day.

•

[Early fall 1970]

HOW I WORK AS A POET

LEW WELCH: We're now recording an inch or two to see if it really works. It doesn't work, you see. Those Japs have failed us again. I really hate electricity. The only reason we have this awful machine at the present time — you must all ignore it, and I think pretty soon we'll all be able to ignore it — is that every time I have a chance to lecture like this, and do it well, there's never a machine; and every time I do it badly, there's always a machine. So I really was kind of ambivalent about this. It probably would have been a lot better if you didn't have the damn thing. But I can really forget that it's there. That doesn't bother me.

And I'm lazy. I've been trying to write an essay — on the subjects I'm going to cover today — for many years, and I can't seem to get it off with just myself and the typewriter in the room because what I'm going to talk about today is really a part of everything and it all gets too large, and I get bogged down in digressions and the damned thing ends up as long as *Tristram Shandy* but not near as much fun. And having the presence of people in the room and some kind of a time limit often is an extremely useful thing. And then I hope that some day or other I'm going to get a decent tape and then I can fool around and try to type it up and everything.

Because there's some stuff I want to talk about today that I've never seen anybody else talk about in exactly the way I think about it — but I don't think that what I'm talking about is particularly original. I think that it's simply the way I take something because of my place in time. But I really believe that every poet that ever worked really thinks something like the way that I think about these particular

subjects we're going to talk about. I'm going to get pretty
technical in this little talk — and by the way, I'm very glad
to be here because it is a very good way to get your own
head straight on something. You know, actually, poetry is
made in a very intuitive way poem by poem, but over the
years you can discern in your habits certain concerns and
cares that you have that make up a kind of a pattern. But
I want to start off with that warning.

Actually I don't think about these things as I'm writing
the poem. I think about the the things we're talking about
sort of in between the writing of the poems. The best way
to keep your head straight about this is a statement by
Gertrude Stein which went, "No one thinks these things
when they are making when they are creating what is the
composition, naturally no one thinks, that is no one form-
ulates until what is to be formulated has been made." You
can really get your head messed around, in a university
situation especially, with the idea of critical standards being
the beginning of a creative work. They actually come after
the work has been made. Some scholar or wag, or he might
even be a person who is an angry critic of the work, will
come after the thing is all made, standing on its pedestal
stuck in the lawn forever; and then he will tell you how it
was made. And the guy that made it is frequently quite surprised to see how clever he was and how many things were going on in the making of this thing which probably was just a
case of here's a big chunk of marble, and he wanted to do
something, and he looked at the marble and he said, "Well,
I can't make a bull out of it because it ought to stand
straight up and bulls stand sideways, so I'll make a mermaid
or something else." And then he starts whacking away at it
and tearing it apart and then the thing sort of takes over by
itself and the — as sculptors often say — the marble began
to tell him where to put the cuts and so on. Maybe it has a
crack in it, and so on. And finally it's all done, and it looks

very much like everything else he's done for the last thirty-five years, because he does have a lot of chops and he does have some standards. But largely they're unconscious.

Now I was overeducated at this university and several others, and so I've always tried to be as conscious about what I do at the same time that I try to keep that from getting in my way. Philip Whalen said once in a letter that the main moral and ethical problem, the spiritual problem, that we have, is learning how to get out of our own way. But then Gertrude Stein also said something that I think is very, very beautiful: "The most delightful state of achievement or state of mind is to know yourself knowing something." It's really nice to really get carried away and dance very beautifully some night and have all your friends tell you, "Gee, you were just too much last night." That's nice. But it's also very sad when you realize that you haven't the slightest idea what you did. It's even more so when you sing or lecture or something. Years later people will say, "Well, you've said so-and-so and such-and-such. And that always impressed me and I think it's very true." And you hear the person saying it and you say, "Gee, I don't even remember even thinking that. I never heard anything so interesting in my life!" And you wonder, did I really say it? or did he hear you say something you didn't say? or did he put it together funny? — or so on. But anyway when you are at your best you do know yourself knowing it.

And so today let's say that the subject of this lecture is simply, for whatever it's worth, I'd like to tell you how I work as a poet.

Now, the first way I work — the first standard that I have — would start with one of Pound's statements. He said: poetry should be at least as well written as prose. And you know it usually isn't. Really, it isn't.

The second thing is: poetry can only use primary materials. It can't use secondary materials. And we get into a

region here that seems so obvious, and such baby talk, that
you get almost embarrassed talking about it; but apparently
most of the people that call themselves poets don't even
realize that you can't make a poem out of anything except
language — any more than a bricklayer can build a brick wall
out of anything but bricks. And most poets don't have the
slightest idea what language is. Like [T.S.] Eliot does not
know what language is. He can make a statement that Milton
had a bad effect upon the English language. Now this shows
absolute complete ignorance of what language is. Language
is speech. It's what we use on the street to buy things with,
to try to seduce women with, to sell cars with, to fight with.
That's language. Everything else is a translation of it. Everything in that library, as soon as it's printed, it's a translation
of language. So a poet who goes to the library for the stuff
of his poetry is using something that never existed in the
first place. He can't make a brick wall, because he eschews
bricks.

   Now, this was extremely important to people my age
because, at the time we came upon maturity and the desire
to be poets, American literature was in the hands of a group
of people that called themselves the New Critics — who knew
absolutely nothing about speech and who thought that Eliot
was a better poet than William Carlos Williams, and a whole
lot of other foolish ideas. And we were extremely lonely as
we rattled around from twenty to twenty-eight years old in
the various universities on our GI Bills. Sure, we were certain that there was such a thing as poet as hero, poet as sage,
poet as shaman, poet as priest, poet as arbiter to the king —
that it was the person in the community who used the language to its finest degree; and that language, which is speech,
is the most powerful single thing that human beings have.
So it's a very high order. And when you read people like
Cleanth Brooks talking about it, and they're the big muckety-
mucks, and you're only twenty-two and you don't have any

ammunition to fight back with, you just get sickened by this
terrible academic dry-ball nonsense in *Partisan Review*. And
reading Eliot is really the most depressing thing in the world
ultimately. And Pound really doesn't leave us any poems. So
we were just all alone, and read our Blake and our Chaucer
and Li Po and Patchen and Miller and the other true poets
of the world like Bobby Burns and so on, and William Carlos
Williams, of course — he was our father; and proceeded to try
to get our skills together so that we could eventually contend
with these gentlemen who to our mind were the absolute
epitome of the antipoet.

Well, let's start with how I went about it here at Reed.
If language is speech, then you have to go out in the street
and listen a lot. *You have to go out in the street and listen
a lot. Da da da da dahdeleedah dadaadeleedah.* You try to
make patterns out of it. So I wrote actually abstract poetry
for quite a long time trying to isolate — *abstract poetry for
quite a long time trying to isolate* . . . that isn't British you
see, it's not British at all — trying to isolate what it was that
we did our business with as Americans. And I got to poems
— I'll give you a couple of examples. Ah, like some of them
only meant, "This is what your speech sounds like." *Da da
da da dee da da.* See, all that trochee, iamb, crap — forget it.
It doesn't have anything to do with us.

Okay, here's one. I call it "Rinse for the Ear":

> To make you hear the
> rhythm of your native speech
> all I can say is
>
> duffer coat equivalent to parka.
> That's the clip of your speech:
> duffer coat equivalent to parka.

> I have to fix and mend my shutters,
> that'll take a whole day,
> that'll take a whole day, too.

Now here's another one. This one's called "Song in Subway: Another Rinse":

> He said there was no music
> in American speech or American scene
>
> at which the lights in the subway tunnel
> were not lights passing in the subway tunnel
>
> became lights thrown by
> spangles on that lady's hat.

Hey?

Now, William Carlos Williams and Gertrude Stein and Hemingway and Scott Fitzgerald and Sherwood Anderson were all working with these things around 1908 on. The reason that they could start working with that at this time was that for the first time in history, the first time in the world, there *was* such a thing as American speech. Whitman had no language to write in. If you read Whitman with this in mind you'll notice these incredible clumsy frenchified funny words. It's just amazing that the man wrote such great, you know, really, world poetry, when he had no language to work in. He just had a hodgepodge. He's like working in the rubble of Europe, and he's sitting in the smokes of industrial America. Wow, how he ever put anything together out of that is a sign of his true greatness.

But then Sherwood Anderson, according to Gertrude Stein, wrote the first really American sentence. I disagree with her. I think that in *Life on the Mississippi* Mark Twain did it. There are certain passages that I've read to people — I said, "Jack Kerouac wrote a passage about the Mississippi

River that never got published and I've got it in manuscript
and I'd like to read it to you." And everybody believed it
was Kerouac, and he [Twain] wrote it about 1886. It's
interesting to read *Life on the Mississippi* with that in mind,
but only read the first half. From then on it's just garbage.
He wrote it until he was thirty-five and then he turned into
funny-man Mark who went around getting drunk and smok-
ing cigars and wisecracking and he became a very bad writer
after he was about thirty-five years old, except for a few
remarkable achievements like that one about *The Mysterious
Stranger* — a real science fiction story, really nice. It came
right at the end of his life. But personal problems got in the
way of his genius and you can see it nowhere better than in
the end of *Life on the Mississippi* as compared to the first
part. There are passages, long Faulknerian-type sentences
that go on two and-a-half pages long and really ring, like the
speech we hear in the street and the speech we actually use.

All right. So now I'm trying to isolate this, as a beginning poet, and the ear became tuned to certain things. Like
I remember we were here on the campus at Reed and we
were talking about sundials and somebody said that they're
more accurate than clocks — and I said they're not more
accurate than clocks unless you have a good compass because
if you set it in your garden wrong to the compass, you can't
keep time. And this girl said, "Oh! There is, then, no unanimity of sundials?" [*Raps twice. Audience laughs.*] And
you really hear that, see, that's interesting. Most of the stuff
you hear, like all day, all day long, all you hear is, "raprap
rapraprap." Everybody's talking, man, from the time they're
this tall until they die, and you never hear anything as interesting as "unanimity of sundials." [*Laughter.*] Except from
somebody who has the gift of ear and tongue that we call
glibness — or among my ancestors, it's blarney, right?

Now, if you don't have glibness, you're never going to
be a writer, because — well, it's like having a tin ear. How in

the world can you ever be a musician if you've got a tin ear?

Well, so anyway Philip Whalen and I were both interested — especially Whalen and I — but, a great great many really good writers found in Gertrude Stein the real abstract work. It's as if Gertrude Stein went out there and took this language that we call American speech and tore it apart and put it back together sort of like an abstract painting, and isolated it; and for Whalen and me especially, and Robert Duncan is another great student of Stein and so is John Cage (who is now a writer and not a musician) — she had an absolutely impeccable ear, and she wrote a book called *How to Write*, and it has sentences like this in it: "Howard means nothing nothing at all in adding in in in English." No — *no* punctuation. You just read page after page of this stuff and there's no punctuation at all, except periods and capitals. "Howard means nothing nothing at all in adding in in in English." Three *ins*, isn't that weird? Or dig this one: "A seated pigeon turned makes sculpture." See, the interesting thing about that one is, you don't know where the verb is until the very end. *A seated pigeon turned* — that's a sentence. Then you say *makes*, and *turned* is not a verb anymore . . . Now, it's really extraordinary how a lot of people can hear that forty-five times and never hear anything. It's like playing a Charlie Parker riff to them. They say, "Huh? They're all wrong notes." Or then other people will say, "Wow!" It's right to them. And so on.

And you can train yourself to get more and more alert to these curious things which really have something to do with our American heritage and our American music: like Philip Whalen's "with your finger on the throttle/ & your foot upon the treadle of the clutch."* A lot of people say, "How can you have your finger on the throttle?" Well, see, cars used to have a throttle, a little button. Then Detroit

* From Whalen's "Self-Portrait, from Another Direction," *On Bear's Head*, p. 74.

came out with a big smash TV advertisement about 1967
about how Oldsmobile is the only car in the world that has
an automatic pilot. Only this is the old finger throttle. You're
going to go to Chicago and you're in Nevada and you just
pull the damned thing out so it hangs at seventy-five and you
just sit there. All the cars used to have it. So, "with your finger on the throttle/ & your foot upon the treadle of the
clutch." Or, I'm going to take a bath in a mountain cabin
and I say, "Every Kettle Pot and Tub."*

Now I can see that most of you aren't hearing any of
this. Well, you hear "bee-loud glade." You say, "Oh gosh,
that's pretty poetry." And you hear, "willow worn of forlorn paramours" — Spenser. [*Laughter.*] I'm telling you,
man, "with your finger on the throttle/ & your foot upon
the treadle of the clutch," is way more interesting than those
two, for all of you, but you got mud in your ears because
you got your ear full of a library, you know what — and the
whole thing about what a poem is gets blurred when you go
to college. It's really bad for you.

Now. Here — all right, you got "willow worn of forlorn
paramours," by Spenser. Dig this one from William Burroughs:
"Motel, motel, motel loneliness blows across the continent
like foghorns blowing over still oily tidal water rivers." Isn't
that neat? [*Laughter.*] And Burroughs can say things like,
"appalling turnstile." [*Laughter.*] He's really the master. Oh,
good, now see? Burroughs got to you right away. [*Laughter.*]

Earlier we were talking about the difference between
American and British English; now, this is nowhere clearer
seen than if you try to read Eliot's essays in American speech.
And remember, Eliot was born in St. Louis, and there's just
no way a kid from St. Louie can talk like Eliot unless he is
a fraud. [*Laughter.*] — A pedant. And he's not even a real
Britisher, see, he's *just* a pedant. But take a guy like Keats in

* From "Preface to Hermit Poems, The Bath," *Ring of Bone*, p. 67.

"La Belle Dame sans Merci." We were trying to remember —
who remembers the last two lines of it? It's something — "the
sedge has wither'd from the lake,/ And no birds sing." Remember? Do you know that poem? Well anyway, he says,
"And no birds sing." You can't say that in American. No
poet would ever say, "birds sing." He'd say, "bird sings."
Bird sings. Birds sing. Birds sing. The British would say, "and
no birds sing." There's a hiatus. Keats wasn't wrong, but
that's a real error, to say "birds sing" if you're an American
poet. It's wrong because you can't say it. In other words,
it's like playing with a bad reed. No musician would ever
make mistakes like that. Why are poets so sloppy?

All right. Now then, because of that you get a lot of
things about how you're never supposed to use too many
sibilants and so on. Just for fun I tried to really do it one
day — I'm so proud of this:

> Apparently wasps
> work all their only summer at the nest,
> so that new wasps work
> all their only summer at the nest,
> et cetera.

See, *wasps work* — *wasps work* is really tough. [*Laughs.*]
See, I wanted to see if I could make *wasps work* and put it
into a poem. Because it's interesting, you know. I think I
did it. It took me quite a while.

> Apparently a wasp
> works all his only summer at the nest,

That'd be one way of doing it. But — *Apparently wasps work*
— that was tough. I said, "Ah, let's try that. Let's make that
work."

Apparently wasps
work all their only summer at the nest,
so that new wasps work
all their only summer at the nest,
et cetera.

Now let's get back to where we started. Poetry has to
be at least as well written as prose. Or let's put it even
tougher. It ought to be as interesting as any conversation.
And it really very rarely is, because — I'm becoming
more and more convinced that the great lesson that William
Carlos Williams taught everybody has been misinterpreted.
He didn't tell you to be dull. He just said, don't be artsy-
fartsy, don't copy the British, write in your own speech
about your own true experience. Let's not have any more
unicorns and maidens. There aren't any maidens in California. There's supposed to be one in Texas who can outrun
her brothers — [*Laughter.*] Anyway, but anyone that uses
maiden in a poem is a pedant. We never use the word except
in horse races. You could have a maiden filly. That means
she never won a race. That's the only time the word is ever
used. And poetry — you know, like, "Oh, I'm going to write
a poem. I'm in love with this girl. Let's see: 'O Maiden . . .' "
Right away! You know, lost!

Now let's get some more. I'm just going to hammer
these at you until you start hearing them. All right. Oh,
here's one by a British guy. Walter Pater said something
that's an example of how words have to work if you're
going to make a poem. He wanted for years and years to
see a certain very beautiful little chapel in France, and he
went to a great deal of trouble to find it and he said, "I
found it and alas, it was utterly restored." See how that
works? *Utterly restored.* Certain words are clichés because
they're only used with certain other words. They never
appear alone. We only say, *utterly destroyed.* We never put

restored against *utterly*. So when he does that, all of a sudden the language, as I often think about it, becomes opaque.

See, usually in the course of our lives we want our language to be such that people see directly through it like a clean window, and get to our meaning. You say, "Mrs. Johnson, I want to buy a steak." And all you want is the steak. You don't want Mrs. Johnson to say, "Wow. How glib." [*Laughter.*] But when you're a poet you do want that. I mean you have to have some reason to put the stuff down on the page so that it doesn't reach margin to margin — that's a definition of poetry I really love. "Poetry is that language which when written does not reach from margin to margin." [*Laughs.*] All right, so you do that.

Well, you got to have some right to confront people with such an oddly spaced bunch of ink. So the words ought to be interesting. You've got to get them interesting. Now they have to be interesting in the way that street talk is interesting because everything else is phony. Because you do have work to do with your poem, too, just like buying the steak; but in the case of the poem you want it also to be brought out — you want the statement to be memorable or delightful or musical or something, at the same time that it's doing its other work.

Now, the apparent plainness of William Carlos Williams has apparently destroyed the feeble ear of the few people that really read it at all anyway, and they think, "Oh! That's how you do it." And then you get a poem that goes:

> A little old lady
> got on the bus
> and gave the bus driver
> her change.

Now isn't that fascinating. [*Laughter.*]

> I had a lady
> that lived next door
> that always hung her laundry
> on the line
> and when the wind blew
> it went flap flap.

You know what I'm talking about, man. You've read the little magazines and you've read all the professor poetry. It's *dull*, man! It's really bad! It's not interesting! [*Laughs.*] The only thing that they've learned, apparently, is: they are blameless now. It really used to be bad, like around 1916, you know:

> Oh, Maiden, by the wells flourishing . . .
> Blah blah blah blah . . .

[*Laughter.*] You know, that's really bad. Now it's blameless:

> I saw a girl
> by the Columbia.

[*Laughter.*] Columbia haiku. [*Laughter.*] It's not a haiku, man! It's not as interesting as any conversation.
     All right, now here's a haiku that I wrote — [*Laughter*] — that I'm very fond of. You know those nasty orange slugs? You know them? I have immortalized them. [*Laughter.*] It's called "Redwood Haiku."

> Orange, the brilliant slug —
> Nibbling at the leaves of
> Trillium

Okay?
AUDIENCE: Okay.

LW: You know, anyone can say

> I saw a yellow slug
> nibbling at a flower.
> It had three petals.

And I'm telling you that — in other words, that the wild
thing about it is if you're a poet, your material, unlike a
carpenter's — See, he has to go to the lumber yard to get
the wood that was cut by the logger that was sent to the
mill that was milled into the right sizes and it's now in a
hardware store and he can now nail it together and make a
house out of it for you. The poet has his material absolutely
free. It's coming out of the mouth of every American in the
whole world. All he has to do is clean his ear out, listen to
it, and put down what he has on his mind out of that material, because there is no other material.

Okay, I'll give you an example of four of them I
wrote here at Reed in 1950. I decided to do a bunch of
abstract poems on the seasons to isolate this language.
"Spring" goes:

> do with hills
> with a pale branch do
>
> do with hills and
> do with every dale
>
> for every single pale pale
> tulip
> a rhododendron
> done
>
> wrench a branch do
> do wrench a branch do
>
> do

Okay. Then, "Winter" was my favorite:

> Alice Herlihy had hard hands
> had hands made hard by
> working for her father with stones
>
> it seemed as though the
> stones would grow from the land
> in wintertime
> to be gathered as a crop and
> stacked into neat low walls
> lacing the land
> separating flocks
>
> Alice used to also sit and sew
> sitting in a little wooden rocking chair
>
> which creaked.

Now you see, that's Monk. Thelonious Monk is making jazz out of the same music that I'm making my poetry out of. I love Thelonious Monk because I know just what he's doing, because that's just what I'm doing. See, *Alice used to also sit and sew, bahpah batten dappoo battendaa. Baphaddatten-deepoodaa. Boo daa.* And it's right there. It's right there in the street. It's cranked up funny, super-intensified and so on. You won't hear people really talk like that, but you might say they're tending toward it and what you do is you just kind of distill it *just* a little bit and then you make it have that kind of interest.

All right then, now let us see. "Summer" was neat:

> nine golden mistresses
> one weaving bees in her hair
>
> with silk
> and with the wings thereof
> she fashioned 20 bunches

>   then she had a perfect ring
>
>   a star

And then "Fall" was:

>   wet
>   the dead leaves stick upon the hillside
>
>   among them
>   beads of a light rain
>   gathered in her short-cropped hair
>   the lean girl walks
>
>   tweeds
>
>   befitting her.
>
>
>   Break not upon a 4-foot hedge the
>   crisp leaf dangling
>
>   shallowly the river flows

Now, that's a very characteristic American thing: *stick upon the hillside. Kettle Pot and Tub. finger on the throttle / & your foot upon the treadle of the clutch.* You hear that? You very rarely see it in professor poetry or the little magazines or anything, because William Carlos Williams didn't have it. He wasn't a musician, he was an imagist, but he had a perfect ear for speech and [his poetry is] really very nice, but he plays down the music of it so much that it's really not there to any considerable degree.

    And I always saw my place and Whalen's place — Whalen sees his in this way too; I know this from conversation — we wanted to put a little more of the music — *a little more of the music*, see, *bah dee badaa n deedap.* It's all bop! Bop didn't come out of nowhere. And you can sing bop right on top of bluegrass banjo picking and it fits just perfectly. And bluegrass is also very close to the way we talk. Anyway, we wanted to isolate and emphasize this kind of music while still being true to Williams', you know, very stern way, very stark way of talking about the things that he had on his mind without really a lot of ego posturing and the other things that make most poetry so distasteful. We wanted to stay plain and at the same time make it as interesting as Parker blowing on his horn.

Now you take something like *Alice Herlihy had hard hands* and so forth, that doesn't need any music to become musical. Now, certain other songs need the tune in order to make it. If you take the lyric out and type it on a page, it looks pretty ridiculous. Bob Dylan is one of the most remarkable poets now working in America, and one of the few great songwriters whose work can be typed up on the page and still looks just fine. It really does. Not every one of them — but some of them are astounding when you see them just flat; and if you look at his music, it's really dull, especially early Dylan. It's really more of a chant then music. Like those — I'm thinking of things like, is it "Highway 61 Revisited" — and the nightmare thing — what was that? "Bob Dylan's 115th Dream"? And it's talking about Columbus and Captain Arab, and "his foot came through the line" — real surreal stuff. It works beautifully on the page. It's really interesting. Every two words is interesting. "Lay Lady Lay" is interesting on the page. That makes a nice little ballad as a printed ballad. But then the majority of — especially the early Dylan — I think his new work really uses the music to a much better degree than earlier. He was really sort of *"whaanaa naa naa naa naa noo noo noo nay noo nay nay nay nay."* It had a hill-country nice thing about it, but musically absolutely dull. Without the words, stupid.

Now then, a lot of songs are stupid without the music. But I think now Leonard Cohen is writing some true poetry

which is also sung. You can take "Suzanne" and type it on
the page and it's interesting — a heck of a lot more interesting
than most of the stuff that people quite pretentiously call
poetry and put in little magazines and so on.

But then there are some songs that are really good songs
that are no good at all without the music. Now, one of mine
goes — [*Sings, to a bop tune* "Supermarket Song"]:

Super Anahist cough syrup tastes as good as the syrup
they put on ice cream [*three times*]

Let's take out the car and park it
At the big, new, supermarket,
And go on inside and see
What they've got for you and me!

Look at all the brand names!
Aren't they really grand names?
Continental Can Corporation of America
Has arranged that to be.

Pepsi-Cola, Coca-Cola, Rice Crispies, and Del Monte,
Best foods   Best foods   Best foods

Everything is wrapped in plastic
Everything begins to look like it came from L.A.

And they
Deal out the Pineapple Dole
To better enable us to meet our role
As customers

In the big, new
Supermarket,

Where we take our car and we park it,
And the bread will never rot, [*laughter*]
And you've got to

Save the stamps, save the stamps,

It's fun!

[*Laughter, applause.*] See, that really needs the tune. You
can't make it work on the page.

And here's another one that really needs the tune.
I sang this to Diz and he said, "Why you got a hit, there."
[*Laughter.*] I always wanted to praise people who write
on shithouse walls. *People who write on shithouse walls —*
you hear that? That's American speech, baapaa baapa doodn
dah. Do you ever see it in poetry? It's amazing. Okay, so, I
never forget it — one day I was fooling around with a guitar
player on a houseboat in Sausalito and we all got very high
and we made about eighteen songs that day. Man, one day.
We made up "Supermarket" that day and this one — and
they're the only two that we remember. We made one for
every sign of the zodiac. [*Laughter.*] As everyone came in
the room, we'd say, "What sign are you?", you know. I
remember [*sings*]:

Aries
Goat on the hill [*laughter*]
Bang, bang, bang.
You will be . . .

And so on. Funny, man. But we forgot it all. [*Laughter.*]
But we had a steel houseboat, and I wrote down "Supermarket" and "Graffiti" on it, and the next day came down
and tried to remember the tune and reworked it and everything, so "Supermarket" got settled, and then this one. Now,
this is a cappella. "Supermarket" can have orchestration with
it [*laughter*], but "Graffiti" is just a guy with a high-hat, like
Lenny Bruce used to do when he said — did you ever hear his
great lecture on "Come"? He says, "You know, there's all

these dirty words . . ." They're going [*imitates drummer using brushes on high-hat*] *shee-datta, shee-datta, shee-datta* — he says, " . . . like you take a word like *come* — 'have you come yet?' [*tapping*] 'yuh gonna come, honey?' To come. 'Oh, I came so good.' Come. Come. Come." It goes on like that. [*Laughter.*] Well anyway, it's really weird, man, and it's beautiful, really beautiful. Because *come* isn't a dirty word — is it? [*Laughter.*] But anyway, "Graffiti" goes — with a high-hat [*imitates drum beat and sings*]:

Graffiti
of the world unite
the world

write
on every wall in sight

fuck   shit   piss   screw
I love you

Big heart
pierced thru
by an arrow.

People who write on shit-house walls
roll their shit in little balls
People who read these words of wit
end up eating those balls of shit.

Here I sit all broken hearted
Came to shit and only farted

Five feet nine
One seventy pounds
Nine-inch cock
Make date
Make date

Graffiti
of the world unite
the world

write
on every wall in sight

fuck   shit   piss   screw
I love you

Big heart
pierced thru
by an arrow.

Tina and Eddie are
true lovers
and always be.

[*Laughs.*] Isn't that a funny little song?

Another example now, an example of songs that don't
need music would be Shakespeare's songs in his plays. We all
know them as printed things. "Mistress mine, where are you
roaming? Stay and hear, your true love's coming," and so on.
And if you go through enough scholarship you can sometimes find, but not always, the tunes that were used in Elizabethan days, and it's pretty much like you'd expect: heavy
Purcell-type Elizabethan English music, you know. Well, we
had a modern-dress Shakespeare play here one summer at
Reed, and I got the job of Balthasar [in *Much Ado about
Nothing*]. And I had to sing this song, and I was determined
to set it West Texas style. First I tried to go through the
scholarship and find out how the Elizabethans sang it, and
I got so discouraged I couldn't do it, couldn't find it anywhere, and I read music just horribly anyway. So finally just
as a joke I set it to, like, a West Texas ballad and it fit perfectly because, of course, you know all our hill-country bal-
lads and everything had an Elizabethan origin, both from

England and Scotland. So it's no wonder that our country music does fit these lyrics so well. Let's see if I can remember it. We used a big bad guitar, you know, *Chong, Chong, Chong* [*sings to a country ballad tune*]:

> Sigh no more, ladies, sigh no more,
>   Men were deceivers ever,
> One foot in sea and one on shore,
>   To one thing constant never.
>
> Then sigh not so, but let them go,
>   And be you blithe and bonny,
> Converting all your sounds of woe
>   Into Hey nonny, nonny.
>
> Sing no more ditties, sing no more
>   Of dumps so dull and heavy.
> The fraud of men was ever so,
>   Since summer first was leavy.

[*Laughs.*] It went like that about three verses.

And so then I decided it would be fun to set a lot of Shakespeare, and I came up here in 1960 and some kid said — I was going to do a few of these Shakespeare songs, and he said, "Well, I got the real 'Mistress Mine.'" They had been singing it here for a long time, and they were singing my song, man. It went through an oral tradition. I was really touched, man. It went through an oral tradition for ten years. "Mistress Mine" goes [*sings*]:

> Mistress Mine,
> Where are you roaming,
> Stay and hear,
> Your true love's coming
>
> > *that can sing, both high and low*

Trip no further, pretty sweeting,
Journeys end with lover's greeting,
Every wise man's son doth know

What is love? 'Tis not hereafter.
Present mirth hath present laughter,

what's to come, is still unsure

In delaying lies no plenty,
Then come kiss me, sweet and twenty,
Youth's a stuff will not endure.

Now, Ginsberg is working — setting Blake. Have any of
you heard those [songs]? They are very interesting.
And let's see. I've just about covered all of this bit that
I was going to do, except to say that when Snyder was here
he wrote a very great ballad with the refrain: "O sack of
batshit-o," and he had another one — my favorite was,

Well coat my balls with honey
and turn me loose in a room
with a hungry bear.

[*Laughter.*] And I remember one, again from Spenser — he
had a line that I always thought was very pretty: "She baréd
her bosom," and I put it in one of my poems.
The trouble is, now, when you want to have your poem
go in and out of, uh, let's see, I don't think Louise put this
one in here — no. Well, I wrote a poem, "My History as an
English Major," in which I have a lot of songs. And you see,
you don't want to put music on the page, because most people
that read poetry can't read music anyway. So I invented the
device of putting musical notes before and after the parts
that were intended to be sung, see. I wanted the device on
the page to be an eighth note and then the poem like this

[*writing on board*] and that — the eighth note would stand for: "the following passage to be sung." And we discovered there is no eighth note in common type. There's only a six-teenth, see, like that. Because — did you ever wonder how music gets printed?

How can you have a machine, man, that can put these notes here, here, here? And all the various flags, and little sharps and flats — it's really weird. And they've got these machines — they have every note, every conceivable note in the Bach system — and it's all Bach, of course — like that. See? Then they have plain bars. So like if that's all you have and you have a rest, and it's on a line, say, it's like that — but then you have to have another eighth note and a bar like this and this — you might want to put it here. Well, I didn't want anything with a couple of bars in it. I just wanted *that*. [*Laughter.*] And we were too poor to draw it and photolithograph it, or make a plate out of it and every-thing. But I know who's copying me, because hundreds of poets are now using sixteenth notes, and that's wrong. [*Laughter.*] So the only place they could have got it is from my book, right? It's neat. Oh, I feel so good. I say, "Well, there's another guy." [*Laughter.*] Because no one — I mean, it's an ugly device. Look how ugly it looks. [*Laughter.*] It's terrible. No one in his right mind would ever use a sixteenth note. I wanted an eighth. It's pretty, it's got a little flag on it.

But this one was from Spenser; the line was "She baréd her bosom," and it goes [*sings*]:

> She baréd her bosom,
> I whupped out m' knife
> Carved my initials
> On her thin breast bone.
> She wept and she cried
> And wrung her pretty hands,

> I said, don't cry my darling
> That's the mark of a man,
> Mark of a man . . .

And so on. [*Laughter.*] I never could get a second verse to come up to that. I always was going to write a real long ballad for it. Never got it.

I'm taking vitamins — these are really not speed. [*Laughter.*]

Well, all right, let's — I'll show you how a person with an ear can do something impossible. We had a game — Snyder and Whalen and I invented it, and it was called the Oswald Spengler — Adelaide Crapsy Mutual Admiration Poetaster's Society. And the game started by — we were sitting around talking about how everybody says that people have a vocabulary of fifteen thousand words and college students—no, five thousand words—and college students have a vocabulary of fifteen thousand, and I know that's utter bullshit. That you couldn't even get through Reed with less than fifty thousand. [*Laughter.*] Really, you couldn't. You just couldn't do it. I've proved it — anybody can do it. Take an ordinary collegiate dictionary and find out how many words it has in it and take a hundred pages at random and find out how many words you don't know. Find the percentage and take it against the total and you'd be amazed. Everybody in this room has a vocabulary of sixty to eighty thousand. Shakespeare used, I think, two hundred and fifty thousand; they've got these creep scholars that count words . . . [*Laughter.*] And Joyce, God! [*Laughter.*] With Joyce it's incredible because he's got all these portmanteau words, and made-up words, and so on, it's just wild. I mean any literate person has a hundred thousand or more. In order to be an educated Chinese you have to have a hundred thousand characters, and characters aren't any harder than words.

Well, so anyway, from that we decided that the trouble

is — most of the words are in what's called your passive
vocabulary. You can read them and understand them, but
you never use them. But if you ever use the word in a poem,
it becomes definitely part of your active vocabulary because
you had to work it so hard to fit it in there, see. Like the
first time you had a four-by-sixteen. You'll never forget the
four-by-sixteen, right?

So, we were just bored, and we decided: let's go through
the dictionary and find five words that none of us know —
and dig, we all have fifty thousand vocabularies and they're
not the same, so there's not going to be very many words
left. There's only three hundred and sixty thousand in the
big one. And it was true. We just couldn't find any word that
nobody — didn't know, except these five. Look at these.
[*Writes on board.*] Does anybody know what that means?
Flamen. Uh, this is a beauty, man. *Liripipionated.* [*Laughter.*]
No kidding. Means hooded, wearing a hood [with a long tail].
That's all it means. Isn't it a pity? Such a big word. Anybody
know what that is? It's [*bema*] pronounced *beema*. It's the
[enclosed area surrounding the altar] in a cathedral. Then —
we couldn't find very many words. Look how weird they
are. So we allowed *geode* because everybody had never used
it. Everybody now — a lot of you know *geode*, don't you?
Hollow rock crystal. Right. And *propolis.* Everybody knew
that, but it was so pretty — [*laughter*]. So you see we weren't
very strict. All right, there's the five words. This is a Roman
priest devoted to but one god. This is hooded. This is that
[area around the altar] in a cathedral. Hollow rock crystal.
And bee [glue]. And we had fifteen minutes to make a poem
using all those words. [*Laughter.*] And Whalen comes up
with:

> Sated flamen
> Liripipionated
> Paces, chanting, in the bema

While demented hillside bees
Pack geodes with propolis and honey—
Sweet rock eggs
Tribute to no walking god

[*Laughter.*] Isn't that incredible? Wow. Boy, that guy really
has it. That Whalen really is so good you just can't believe it.
  Now, all right, so let's put it this way. All that I've been
talking about so far is what you do, or what I did, as a very
young man with really not very much to say — trying to get
the toolbox together and get my materials ready, so that if
I had something to say, I'd be able to do it, you see? And
then as I got older I had things to say, that I wanted to say,
and sometimes the writing of the poem was ridiculously easy.
Other times it took a long time.
  Now, "Wobbly Rock" is an interesting poem from the
standpoint of how it was made. I had just left my first wife
and I went out to this rock at Muir Beach and I sat down
there to think everything over. It was a foggy and windy day.
And I got this whole poem simultaneously. Mozart reports
this — not that I'm trying to compare myself with Mozart,
but we have a mind of the same order structurally — Mozart
reports that he got all of his symphonies instantaneously.
And he said — this was in a letter to one of his friends — he
says, that sounds ridiculous since there is no way of thinking
of music outside of the duration of time. But he says, you
get the symphony, whup!, the whole thing, see. He says,
then I have to go home and there's all this tiresome business
of putting all those little black notes down. It's kind of interesting insight into the way Mozart's mind worked.
  Well, I had the same experience with this one. I got
it instantaneously and it took me three-and-a-half years to
get all the little black notes down. Like, some days I'd say,
"Oh that's what goes in that fourth section there. *Da-da-da-
da-da.*" One line. And sometimes a whole section would

come. But it was all done. There was no fun in writing the
thing, it was — it had all been done already. I just didn't
have the words to put in there yet, which again sounds
ridiculous, but I'm just reporting what happened. And then
there's — all right, so the first stanza goes:

> It's a real rock
>
> > (believe this first)
>
> Resting on actual sand at the surf's edge:
> Muir Beach, California
>
> > (like everything else I have
> > somebody showed it to me and I found it
> > by myself)
>
> Hard common stone
> Size of the largest haystack
> It moves when hit by waves
> Actually shudders
>
> > (even a good gust of wind will do it
> > if you sit real still and keep your mouth shut)
>
> Notched to certain center it
> Yields and then comes back to it:
>
> Wobbly tons

I sent this [to my sister], this was my first book that
was published, it was just this one poem, and my sister said,
"Well, I guess it's all right, but I don't understand it." Now,
look to the lengths I went, man. *It's a real rock.* [*Laughter.*]
Do you know what *it's* means? *a* means, *real* means, *rock*
means? Then to make sure, I say, parenthesis, *believe this
first.* And she says, "What does that mean?" [*Laughter.*]

And she's not dumb. So, with this poem I really gave up. I
mean, now I just write whatever — I don't try to help anybody any more. [*Laughter.*] *Resting on actual sand at the
surf's edge* colon. And then, where? *Muir Beach, California.*
[*Laughter.*] "I don't understand it." God! And then they
say, "How big is it?" Like, Whalen said, "What do you mean?"
he said, "Hard common stone / size of the largest haystack."
You know, "Is it a little rock, is it a big rock . . . ?" It was
very discouraging, man. Like, I really said, "All right, I'm
going to crank it up —" this came out about 1960. I said,
"I'm going to make something so plain that nobody can
miss it." "What does it mean?" So if any of you are working
with poetry, don't worry about that. It'll just destroy you.
It'll break your heart.

Okay. Now we know where it is. It's a rock. You sit on
it and it wobbles. [*Laughter.*] Whew! "I don't understand it."
Now, everybody that's ever been to the beach has sat on a
rock that wobbles. Really, it happens all the time. The sand
shifts and the thing goes *Clunk. Clunk.* It's really kind of
neat. Wobbly rock means that, like it says. [*Laughter.*] Okay.
Now, [stanza] 2, it says:

> Sitting here you look below to other rocks
> Precisely placed as rocks of Ryoanji:

Now, that might be difficult, but probably most of you
know — one of the most famous gardens in Japan is Ryoanji.
It's made entirely of gravel and has, I believe, fifteen stones
in it — they're in five groups.

> Foam like swept stones

Now this gets a little complicated:

> (the mind getting it all confused again:
> "snow like frosting on a cake"
> "rose so beautiful it don't look real")

All right, the poet has said the foam is like swept stones.
Well actually the swept stones is like foam, right? Now why
do we have the word *frosting* for a cake? Because it looks
like frost. But it isn't. So if you say, "snow like frosting on
a cake," you're getting it backwards, aren't you? The frosting
on the cake is like snow. And then, that one always got me —
"rose so beautiful it don't look real." I'm sure you've all
heard that. *Oh my goodness, she's so beautiful she don't
look real.* What do you want, a plastic doll?

> Isn't there a clear example here —
> Stone garden shown to me by
> Berkeley painter I never met
> A thousand books and somebody else's
>   boatride ROCKS
>
>   (garden)
>
> EYE
>
>   (nearly empty despite this clutter-image all
>   the opposites cancelling out a
>   CIRCULAR process: *Frosting-snow*)

You see, actually, it's a valid insight. You look at the snow,
and you think — it's like frosting on a cake, and then you
realize that the frosting on the cake came from snow, and
then you see a nice yin-yang circle, and you get to a nice
empty mind.

> Or think of the monks who made it

—that's Ryoanji —

                                        450 years ago
                    Lugged the boulders from the sea
                    Swept to foam original gravelstone from sea

                    (And saw it, even then, when —

—It should say, *and saw it first,* — shouldn't it? Dan typed
this up and made typos all over the place. [*Laughter.*] What
does it really say? It should say, *saw it, even then* — does it?
— *when finally they all* — — that should say *first,* in there,
somewhere. That's an error on my part, seriously. See, that's
not clear. *First* — I would now write it:

                    (First saw it, even then, when finally they
                             all looked up
                    the moment —

I'm sure it says *instant.* Yeah. Dan! Dan! Dan! you bad pig.
I mean, there's the thing! The care is, is it *moment* or *instant,*
see? Here, there's a difference —

                    AFTER it was made)

— I wanted to quote Stein. She said — one or the other.
[*Laughs.*] Damn it, I don't remember.

                    And now all rocks are different and
                    All the spaces in between

                    (which includes about everything)

> The instant
> After it is made

All right, that's stanza 2. Now, what I'm trying to do there is make a little essay on the creative process. Like I said, you can't think about anything until after it was made. Now, Ryoanji is one of the most impressive things ever made by any human beings anywhere. It is simply gravel and a few rocks on which some moss now grows, and it's made to look like the ocean in that crazy stylized way the Japanese people work. And I'm saying that the monks who made it, the Zen monks who made it, never saw what they were doing until after it was made, and so on. And then I like,

> And now all rocks are different and
> All the spaces in between
>
> (which includes about everything)

— See, most of Ryoanji, like most of Japanese art, is the space left over after the few statements are made, whether it be painting or poetry or gardens or whatever. They have a very nice sense of space, which Western people always fill with blabber. They can't keep quiet, or leave anything out. Like the painters always have to put the big background in, and everything, you know. So that's what that was about.

All right, now the third section has a little joke in it that only I know unless I tell, unless I tell anybody — nobody's ever found it. And it says,

> *I have been in many shapes before I attained*
> *   congenial form*
> All those years on the beach, lifetimes . . .

When I was a boy I used to watch the Pelican:
It always seemed his wings broke
And he dropped, like scissors, in the sea . . .

Night fire flicking the shale cliff
Balls tight as a cat after the cold swim
Her young snatch sandy . . .

> *I have travelled*
> *I have made a circuit*
> *I have lived in 14 cities*
> *I have been a word in a book*
> *I have been a book originally*

Dychymig Dychymig: (riddle me a riddle)

> Waves and the sea. If you
> take away the sea

Tell me what it is

Now the joke is, everything — *I have been in many shapes
before I attained congenial form* — and *I have travelled* and
I have made a circuit, and all those I haves and *Dychymig
Dychymig* are from *Taliesin,* which is a great old poem from
Wales, and this is the history section of this poem, and it's
Old Welch. [*Laughs.*] Isn't it funny — no one ever noticed
it and it doesn't make any difference, but a lot of times you
put in little jokes like that just for your own fun. Anybody
could find that. It's in Robert Graves' *White Goddess.* Isn't
that a great thing? That's from *Taliesin,* "I have been in many
shapes before I attained congenial form."
  Okay, 4 is sociology.

> Yesterday the weather was nice there were lots
> of people

Today it rains, the only other figure is far up the
    beach

    (by the curve of his body I know he leans
        against the
    tug of his fishingline: there is no separation)

Yesterday they gathered and broke gathered and
    broke like
Feeding swallows dipped down to pick up something
    ran back to
Show it
And a young girl with jeans rolled to mid-thigh ran
Splashing in the rain creek

    "They're all so damned happy —
    why can't they admit it?"

—Gary Snyder said that one day while we were walking on
Muir Beach. It's really dreadful to feel bad, and look at all
these happy people who think they feel bad. Oh, man.

Easy enough until a little rain shuts beaches down . . .

Did it mean nothing to you Animal that turns this
Planet to a smokey rock?
Back among your quarrels
How can I remind you of your gentleness?

Jeans are washed
Shells all lost or broken
Driftwood sits in shadow boxes on a
    tracthouse wall

Like swallows you were, gathering
Like people I wish for . . .

    cannot even tell this to that fisherman

Now then we get into the satoris.

> 3 of us in a boat the size of a bathtub · pitching in
> slow waves · fish poles over the side · oars

> We rounded a point of rock and entered a small cove

> Below us:
> > fronds of kelp
> > fish
> > crustaceans
> > eels
>
> Then us
>
> > then rocks at the cliff's base
> > starfish
> > (hundreds of them sunning themselves)
> > final starfish on the highest rock then
>
> Cliff
>
> > 4 feet up the cliff a flower
> > grass
> > further up more grass
> > grass over the cliff's edge
> > branch of pine then

> Far up the sky

> > a hawk

> Clutching to our chip we are jittering in a spectrum
> Hung in the film of this narrow band
> Green
> > to our eyes only

Now there's the music we were talking about. *Clutching to
our chip we are jittering in a spectrum | Hung in the film of
this narrow band | Green | to our eyes only*

On a trail not far from here
Walking in meditation
We entered a dark grove
And I lost all separation in step with the
Eucalyptus as the trail walked back beneath me

Does it need to be that dark or is
Darkness only its occasion
Finding it by ourselves knowing
Of course
Somebody else was there before . . .

I like playing that game
Standing on a high rock looking way out over it all:

"I THINK I'LL CALL IT THE PACIFIC"

Wind water
Wave rock
Sea sand

(there is no separation)

Wind that wets my lips is salt
Sea breaking within me balanced as the
Sea that floods these rocks. Rock
Returning to the sea, easily, as
Sea once rose from it. It
Is a sea rock

(easily)

I am
Rocked by the sea

Like Bill Brown pointed out, he says, "Your whole poemic
reputation rests on a pun." I like puns. They're really neat.
Like in that hiking poem where I say, *you bear with me.*

Let's just put it this way: I have spent a lot of time trying to be really quite careful and thinking about craft in a very specific way. And it's been kind of tiresome and sad, especially to see how the academy — they say, "Oh, Welch, he's just prosy." You know, and I hope I've shown you that one of the tests I make of a line is, I want to read it between clenched teeth. And Jack Spicer, whose poetry is very strange — it's hard for me to understand what he's got on his mind, but they really are very tight, good, strong poems. I always get the impression that he put a bunch of twenty-penny nails in a six-by-twelve and then he proceeded to bite them all off, down the line. [*Laughter.*] And it's really — I guess it's just natural, that the ear of the academy and the people on the street — *the people on the street* — see, it's right there — can't seem to see what the really contemporary poet is trying to do with the really contemporary language. Boccaccio had the same trouble, Chaucer had the same trouble, certainly William Carlos Williams, all those years — nobody thought he was doing anything except the young students, they could, you know, we could always hear it. And anyway, maybe you can hear it a little better — *hear it a little better, ree de de de dee dat*, when you read the poetry of America today and see where the music is at.

See, it's not at rhymes. Rhymes are just stupidly dull. But you can do all kinds of things that are musical with the very language that you do have free — it's just lying right around — and then go about your business of saying what you have on your mind. And if you do it honestly enough, you really do end up with something that's a great pleasure to others and to yourself, you know, for making it.

I want to say it has nothing to do with this business of *express yourself*, you know? There really is something about the whole art that doesn't give a damn about that self thing. And one of the best ways to free yourself from it, and I'm sure it's very tiresome to you too, whatever you call your

ego — if you really want to get rid of it, listen to your Tribe
talk. Listen to the way it goes, and try to get some kind of a
structural ear about it. And then you immediately discover
all of the dance, all of the music, and all of the real meaning
about what your Tribe is trying to do and what the artists of
that Tribe are trying to do, whether they be dancers or
painters or musicians or poets, or anything. And then it becomes very easy to see the difference between the phonies
and the real ones.

You know, Truman Capote has nothing, just nothing,
and it's always the case that some phony like that captures
the tribal ear and it's very depressing, because — like Gertrude Stein used to say: "All the newspapers and magazines
have such fun imitating me and making fun of me." She said,
"If they'd only read the original they'd see I'm a lot funnier
than that." It's really true, too. She's very funny. I used to
just break up. It's real ha ha funny — have to put the book
down because the tears are coming in your eyes, because
she's saying goofy things like:

> A is an article.
> They are usable. They are found and able and edible.
> And so they are predetermined and trimmed.

[*Laughs.*] You know, trying to get the language into an
abstract thing, into an opaque thing, into something that
you can build with.

Then of course when she wanted to do the building
like she did in *Alice Toklas* or *Melanctha*, or any of the others
— or the lectures — it's perfectly clear writing, a whole lot
clearer than all these other idiots. And the reason it's clearer
and it stands up is because it's made out of the primary
material instead of secondary material. It's made out of the
stuff that comes off the street, that comes out of the mouths
of the Tribe itself, and the stuff it carries is the same stuff

that the Tribe carries, and then it becomes of interest and
important and delightful. And if it doesn't have these things,
it can't be interesting at all. And then of course, like Stein
said, she put it this way, "You can only say what you know,
and you can only say what you know in the only way you
know how to say it. Now, of course you can do this perfectly
and nobody will be interested. If so, too bad." Now, she
means something about *know* that's quite a lot different
than what most people say when they mean *know*. She
means, *know yourself knowing it*. And it's just astonishing
how many people talk about stuff they don't know and they
talk about it in a language that they don't know how to
speak, and so of course you end up with absolutely nothing.

Okay. Do you have any questions? I'll be glad to answer
them.

VOICE FROM AUDIENCE: I want to say something about
how you were talking . . . Remember how when you were
trying out some patterns and you said that we weren't
hearing them, and then you tried out a couple . . .

LW: And then the Burroughs, bang!

VOICE: And you said, "Burroughs got you." But, I think
that what got us was you, that you really changed your
style, that —

LW: Maybe so.

VOICE: You see . . . there was much more glory in the
presentation of Burroughs. The other stuff was much more
academic.

LW: Oh yeah. That's a very tricky thing. Yeah, I'm glad you
brought that up. Like somebody said to Stein: "I can't read
anything you wrote because when I read it I always hear you
talking it, and I don't know whether it's because I like you
or I like the writing." See? Now, I found it terribly important,
when I was starting all this, to be able to have the records
that we have. We've got Joyce, Pound, Eliot, Cummings —
almost anybody is on record and you can go — it doesn't

take much trouble — go to the research librarians and get
them off their ass and make them do their work and you
can get a big stack of records.

And for example, I couldn't understand Dylan Thomas
at all. I couldn't get it off the page until I heard him on
the record, and then it was just really easy. I was trying to
make Dylan Thomas mean something quite large. He doesn't.
The whole poem means, "I'm thirty-one." And it's so far
out, the way the language is so dense and musical and everything. You keep trying to make symbols out of things. He
says "seagull," he just means any seagull, or, "there are
seagulls." And all he's saying is, "I'm a poet, I'm thirty-one,
I'm a singer, and I'm standing out here, and I'm damned
glad I'm thirty-one, and man, I'm going to sing!" Though,
I was trying to make it — like the academy teaches you to
try to make it — *mean* something, and I lost what it really
did mean. It means a whole lot more than these tricky little
metaphysical junky poems that, you know, that you have
to really have lots of glosses for and everything to figure
out. That was a perfectly honorable thing to say, "I'm
thirty-one and it's thus-and-so day and here we are in Wales
and I'm perfectly happy about it." I mean that's fine. I'd
been overtaught about this thing, and he was supposed to
be so major. And then as soon as you've heard him read it,
then you pick up the page and always hear him. And he's
just a drunken babble. Just a delightful, wonderful singer.
And it was a ball.

But I remember this [past] summer at Greeley, Colorado — University of Northern Colorado — I was the
resident poet there — and you know the poem of Dylan
Thomas' about the funeral of the old lady, Ann ["After the
Funeral"] ? And he mentions in the poem that they come
into the funeral parlor and he says, "In a room with a stuffed
fox and a stale fern," see? And as we were doing this poem,
I said, "Now, the poet, Thomas, comes into a funeral parlor

and he sees a stuffed fox. Now, isn't that weird? I mean,
isn't that strange, for a funeral director to have a stuffed
fox?" That's all it means. Ann was dead and he was coming
into the room and the poet notices a stuffed fox, and that's
pretty weird. I mean there's a real — you know, a man on
a death trip, the undertaker thing, he's a vulture living off of
death, and he has a stuffed fox. That's all it means, it's a
stuffed fox in a funeral parlor. Then later he says he's going
to keep raging until the lungs of the stuffed fox shout love.
So he makes something of it.

And a kid raised his hand and said, "Gee, last year we
spent three weeks on the symbolism of the stuffed fox."
You know, how it was Loki, it was Mercury, it was, like,
Coyote, it was the trickster hero. It was the poet himself
in death, later, aaaah — No. It's a stuffed fox in the funeral
parlor. That's far enough out, man! [Laughter.] How far
out do you have to get? Or as Cocteau put it — I keep coming
back to it so many times: "The poet does not want to be
understood. He demands to be believed." It's a real rock! /
Resting on actual sand! / Muir Beach! "Uh, I don't understand it." [Laughter.]

Until, you know — now, it has to be that we've been
cheated. Because all through history there have been poets
and all of them have always felt the same. They carry the
news, they warn the prince, they talk about trips, they say
you really should go up to that mountain and watch the
sunset because it's out of sight. And then they say, "Well,
why don't you come up and do it for us on Easter?" And
you say, "Cool." Really. Then you demand to be believed.
You say, "Here comes the sun. It's the only god we've got.
It's shining on the earth. It is our mother. It is a big round
ball." You know, you say things like that. And they say,
"Oh, how symbolic!" [Laughter.] "How surreal." [Laughter.]
Whew! Boy.

And look what we've been fed. We've been fed the

vomiting of death from Europe for a thousand years. There
is the Father, the Son, and the Holy Ghost, we are taught.
The Trinity is the Father, the Son, and the Mother. Everybody knows that, and every Catholic prays only to Mary.
And Paul, who said, "It is better not to marry, but it is
better to marry than to burn," who was a faggot, couldn't
stand to have a woman in the Trinity, so put in the Holy
Ghost. Now who the hell could ever pray to a Holy Ghost?
[*Laughter.*] And then that god-damned book of Hebrew
lies, like Ezra Pound calls it, tells us that Man is the chosen
son of God. So we're better than everybody. So if you see
a tree, cut it down. If it's warm, shoot it! Put all your nitro-
gen in the god-damned river! Shit in the Bay! [*Laughter.*]
Because we're King, man! See, we've been lied to so god-
damned long. Suppose you are a devout Catholic and you
want to pray, and you say to the priest, "Father, what is
the Holy Ghost?" "Ah, my son, mumble, mumble, mumble,
mumble." [*Laughter.*]
VOICE IN AUDIENCE: Turn it over —
LW: No, that's great. What is that, an hour and a half?

[Reed College lecture, 30 March 1971]

LEATHER PRUNES

LEATHER PRUNES

Preface

"Abner Won't be Home for Dinner" is a Leather Prune, a kind of literary structure, a backwards Tender Button.

The term Leather Prune comes from a conversation with Richard Brautigan. "Oh Flap City! Oh those leather wings!" he said. Later he said, "I didn't get your cherry, and I don't want your prune."

Thus "Leather Prune" was given to me as the right name for some of the things I write right now.

Leather Prunes often make clean words dirty, or Lenny Bruce backwards, and tighter. I deeply regret I never had a chance to show him one.

Most Leather Prunes, as this one is, are one-man plays. A man of many voices stands alone on a bare stage and makes a greaseless theater. Since there are no wings, in the set-lumber sense that is, there can be no useless hysteria behind them. Farewell, Judy Garland.

Titles, scene changes, set directions, speakers' names and curtains, are all part of the performed text. Otherwise the timing, the shape, is not revealed.

ABNER WON'T BE HOME FOR DINNER

ACT ONE

SCENE ONE: ABNER *and* JESSIE *seated at a table.*

BERNARD: Is that you Abner?

ABNER: All alone. All alone.

JESSIE: I don't really like birds.

ABNER: They're practically reptiles.

BERNARD: Well, I think I better be going now.
                Thanks a lot.

(exits)

Enter MUSICIANS *and* COURTESANS, *singing:*

                We
                Musicians &
                Courtesans
                Are

SCENE TWO

ABNER: Lost.

JESSIE: What.

ABNER: Lost.

JESSIE: What.

ABNER: Lost.

JESSIE: Lost what?

ABNER: All alone. All alone.

SCENE THREE

ABNER: ThumpThumpThumpThumpThumpThump
                 ThumpThumpThumpThumpThumpThump

JESSIE: How do I know when you're through?

ABNER: ThumpThumpThumpThumpThumpThump
                 Shut up
                 ThumpThumpThumpThumpThumpThump

JESSIE: You never say you love me anymore.

ABNER: Thump, ThumpThump

                 Thump.

SCENE FOUR

BERDETTE: Scrape it out.

ABNER: Scrape scrape.

BERDETTE: Scrape it out.

ABNER: Scrape scrape.

BERDETTE: Scrape it out.

ABNER: Scrape.

(End of Act One & Intermission)

ACT TWO

SCENE ONE: *Merry.*
            Seated at a very long table:

                JOSLIN
                FRED
                BERDETTE
                RUBY
                MUSICIANS & COURTESANS

JOSLIN: Ho ho ho

BERDETTE: You big freak, you brought me down!

RUBY: Far Away. Far Away.   (*swoons*)

BERDETTE: Down I say. You brought me down!
                     (*stamps her foot*)

JOSLIN: May I introduce myself?

FRED: My card?

        (*Exit,* FRED *and* JOSLIN, *arm in arm*)

RUBY   There goes one of the smartest son-of-
(*awakening*):   a-bitches you and me will ever know.
                     (*swoons*)

BERDETTE: Down. The bastard. Brought me down.
                     (*stamping foot*)

        SCENE TWO

ABNER: Computer computer.

BERNARD: Miss Computer to you.

ABNER: ThumpThumpThumpThumpThump
                     ThumpThumpThumpThumpThump

BERNARD: Freak. Freak.

ABNER: ThumpThumpThumpThumpThump
            ThumpThumpThumpThumpThump
            Computer computer.

BERNARD: Freak.

ABNER: ThumpThumpThumpThumpThump
            ThumpThumpThumpThumpThump

BERNARD: All is lost.

ABNER: "What, must our mouths be cold?"

SCENE THREE

ABNER: The branch of wrath.

BERDETTE: Lost wasp?

BERNARD: O broken Arab hasp!

ABNER: Well, I guess I better be going now.
            Thanks a lot.

(exit)

Enter MUSICIANS *and* COURTESANS, *singing:*

Is that you Abner?

SCENE FOUR

ABNER: Scrape scrape.

JESSIE: Is that you Abner?

ABNER: Scrape scrape.

JESSIE: I don't really like birds.

ABNER: Scrape scrape.

JESSIE: They're practically reptiles.

ABNER: Scrape. Thump. Scrape.

(Curtain)

[*O'er*, No. 2, December 1966]

A PLAIN LEATHER PRUNE

Grab Lotion

Nobility bubble

Belly suck

Grope salve

Grope Lotion.

Grab salve.

A LEATHER PRUNE FOR J. EDGAR HOOVER

Probe joy.   Probe joy.   Hire fink.   Probe.
Close up all the holes in every body?
Probe loyal.   Probe loyal.   Grope.

What's that girl doing down the hall.   Anyway.
Probe loyal.   Hire fink.   Probe.
You were late four times this month.
Probe.   Probe loyal.   Probe fink.

Line 'em up, pull their pants down, and make 'em cough.
Grope.   Probe.   Probe loyal.
I don't want to see no hands in any pockets.
Hire fink.   Probe loyal.   Grope.

*Maybe we ought to get him fixed. The last one
sprayed all over the bookcase.*
Probe.

Close up all the holes in every body?
Raincoats and helmet liners.

BABY SUCK

for Dave Meltzer

Fondle bundle. Suck bundle. Baby suck.
Fondle bundle. Drool bundle. Stare.

Suck giggle.
Suck giggle.
Suck giggle.

Sleep.

Are all his bones all right? Even his knees?

What an early thing it is, when a face gets close enough
to laugh!

He flaps his rubber hands around!

Suck sleep.
Suck sleep.
Suck sleep.
Cry.

Fingernails!

Scratch his mother's breast.

BOOTH IS TROOTY

CAST

BOOTH: *John Wilkes Booth masked as*
           John Carradine.

TROOTY: *Jayne Mansfield, played by*
           Aphrodite, masked as Barbara
           Somers: 6'0" tall, who lisps
           (but not cutely).

Stage is bare and unswept. BOOTH, *dressed in Victorian actor outfit, in mid-stage.*

The whole stage is lit. Then, just before BOOTH *speaks, blackout. Then, spotlight on* BOOTH.

BOOTH (*playing with an old dueling pistol*):

> Ah, I see in yonder
> booth a
> President!   And I,
> Booth, on stage, must
> fire into booth.
>
> Iniquity!   Iniquities now
>
> Rampant!   State
> booth-bound!   Target of such
>
> Temptation I

Shoot!

(*shoots*)

All lights turn on, even houselights. TROOTY *runs in.*

TROOTY (*in topless evening dress*):

Booth! Booth! O Booth! O no!

(*aside*)   *I fear it*
                   must be much too
                   late. The bullet
                   finds its mark! The
                   State lies dead in
                   booth!

No, Booth! No! Your target not in
          booth, O

Both of us! O

too late knowing we betray!

Betray!

(*falls into his arms*)

While kissing, & indeed, outrageously groping one
another, TROOTY, *as pointed out, in topless evening*
dress, BOOTH & TROOTY *EXCHANGE MASKS!!!*

They leap apart at the instant of mask-exchange.

BOOTH (*masked as Trooty*):

> What?   What . . . .
>
> Have I done?   O?   O!
>
>   Who?
>
>   in booth lies State
>
> DEAD?
>
> Dead, who once was
>
>   State?   Who once was
>
> "what," not
>
> surely
>
>   Booth! !
>
> was .   .   .   .

TROOTY (*masked as Booth*):

> Iniquity!   Outrage!   O
>
> my ears ring of it, ears
>
>   shall ring
>
> throughout all time!   Smoke
>
>   sting

nostrils,   his

wise brow

bleeding!   His

swelling tongue!

BOOTH (*masked as Trooty. stunned.*):

What instru-
ment now smokes in this
hand?   whose?

whose?   O

Trooty!

Trooty?

TROOTY (*masked as Booth*):

It's true!   It
shot so true!

BOOTH (*masked as Trooty*):

In booth

TROOTY (*removing her mask & flinging it aside*):

I REVEAL MYSELF ! ! ! !

BOOTH (*still masked as Trooty*):

> Truly?

> TROOTY *removes topless evening gown. Stands stark naked before him.*

BOOTH (*covering his still Trooty-masked eyes*):

> I see?
>
> I see!

TROOTY: Off with it!

> Off with every bit of it!
>
> Your gun!
>
> Your gun too, too!

> BOOTH *throws mask aside, removes all clothing, walks, naked, to front of stage, and throws his pistol, gently, into the center aisle. He watches it slide to rest.*
>
> *Then, slowly, with outstretched arms, he staggers toward* TROOTY. TROOTY, *her hands shielding her eyes, rocks to and fro, staggering, slightly backwards.*

TROOTY (*hands over her eyes*):

> Blinding!

> Blinding!

Fierce arc-lights blink on & off, the stage as if in a lightning storm — the brightness really painful.

BOOTH, *despite all this, does not shield eyes.*

BOOTH:	Love!	Love!
TROOTY:	Blind!	Blind!
BOOTH:	Love!	
TROOTY:	Blind!	
BOOTH:	Love!	
TROOTY:	Blind!	Blind!
BOOTH:	O WORLD ENOUGH AND TIME ! ! ! !	

Enormous explosion, as with old-time photographers' flash. Light should be so bright, so sudden, the actors can disappear before the eyes of the audience can readjust.

A bare stage. Unswept.

Curtain.

House lights up. Let applause go on unanswered. Let
confusion in the audience begin. Let purses be found,
glasses cases, coats and programs hugged among
umbrellas, underneath the arm extended to our ladies
rising from their most uncomfortable seats . . . . . .

and then the moment of lull, predictable,

and then a female voice. From the balcony:

VOICE FROM BALCONY:

ABE!

ABE!

(oh,   no   )

— END —

NOTE: *Costumes should have back-zippers or easy*
             thongs, so disrobing can be done as a dance
             quick enough to stay within the beat of the
             play as it goes.

BELLY MUSKY PIT

Throw it away. Throw it away. Put it in an ashcan,
in a paper sack. Flush it. Down.

Right in Macy's Ladies Room?
Right in front of everybody?

Belly. Musky Pit. Throb.
She cut her jeans off short, almost to her groin, and
let the edges fray.

(an almost hurt, an almost sick feeling)

Right in front of everybody?

Right on any streetcorner.

Belly. Musky Pit. Throb.

What if you never got here in the first place, jeans cut
right up to the groin and let the edges fray?

(An almost hurt, an almost sick feeling)

Belly. Musky Pit. Throb.

Right in Macy's Ladies Room?

In a paper sack.

THIRTY THIRTY

A Play. Actually, an Acted-Poem.

> *For Joanne, on her birthday*

Nervously. JOANNE. Arranging, or poking at, her hair. Staring out the window. Humming. A THOUGHT strikes her! (panic) She shrieks.

JOANNE: **THIRTY !?!???!!!**   (*runs to mirror*)

(chants)

> *Dreizig!*
> *frightwig!*
> *On the Wall,*
> *who's the . . . ?*

(shielding her eyes)

        O!   O!   O!

(exits)

A POET: One of our fairest has come, finally,
about a third of the way to,
IF she continues to take good care of
        herself &
LEARNS TO PAY ATTENTION ! ! !

(fades)

JOANNE (*from wings. The voice composed, professional*):

Do I look all right?

FOGHORNS (*a salute*):

THREEEEEE   O

THREEEEEE   O

A VOICE: . . . and   won .   the West

— 30 —

[19 November 1964]

STORIES

THE MAN WHO PLAYED HIMSELF

Jimmy Vahey (say it: Vah-HEE'), when he was younger, played a little Alto. When he was high he also played patterns on a short Marimba. The Marimba was in his room, beside the mirror, ready for pattern-playing while he dressed. "While he dressed" was almost always a very long time.

Jimmy Vahey was impeccable. About two in the afternoon he'd get out of bed. His wife had been up for hours, painting. She had her own little pattern, impeccable and womanly, and Jimmy never intruded. They got exactly together every once in a while, coming to it from different directions, and then made delicate and mutually satisfying love. They always knew exactly where they were, so they always knew the instant they got together. They never pushed it. They never avoided it. They both knew: relation is mutual.

About two in the afternoon Jimmy Vahey got out of bed. The San Francisco sun came perfectly through matchstick bamboo blinds and lit the room where everything was its own, natural, color. Rice-straw rug, Hurricane reed chairs, earth-colors on Mexican raw cotton bedspread, bamboo colors of the Marimba, maple frame of full-length mirror, white walls, white rice-paper Japanese globe hiding the light fixtures.

Jimmy didn't have a hangover, but took three aspirins anyway. The tablets were not buffered or otherwise added to, and sat whitely in a small apothecary jar with a buffed glass stopper. Beside the jar was a half-smoked joint of Marijuana — a cigarette neatly rolled in Bambu paper, the trade name, a brand Jimmy had never been able to find except in a small shop on East 48th Street in New York City. The last time he was in New York he bought two dozen packets of these papers — by long odds the best in the world.

So he had put this joint, or half-joint, beside the aspirin jar there on the glass shelf of the medicine chest, the night before, and there, today, at two o'clock, it was. He lit it and smoked it while taking a shit.

Rice paper covered the bottom half of the bathroom window. The top half of the window was clear glass, clean. Jimmy Vahey watched gulls fly in the bright blue sky of San Francisco. Sweet smoke mingled with the immaculate smell of his offal. A tingle, like a light hand pressing the back of his head, occurred on the third long-held inhalation of the cigarette. He therefore snuffed out the joint and returned the one-quarter-inch roach to its place beside the aspirin jar.

He wiped his ass carefully and watched the smeared white papers whirl and get sucked away by the flushing toilet. Then he washed his anus with warm water and finger tips. Then he carefully washed his hands.

Deciding to take his shower *before* he ate breakfast, he removed his boxer shorts (white, with widely spaced geometric blue figures) and examined himself in the full-length mirror on the inside of the bathroom door. He felt neither love nor aversion for this body of his — it was only what he walked around in, and he liked to keep it up.

He found no pimples, one small blackhead behind his left shoulder. This he squeezed, black top on tiny white cone, regarding it as it sat on the index finger of his right hand. He wiped it onto one page of toilet paper, dropping the toilet paper into the toilet bowl.

While taking his shower, Jimmy Vahey became very hungry and also felt himself coming down. He decided while soaping, to have a full pipe of pot *before* breakfast and *after* drying himself compeletly. The shower, therefore, was not perfect — was, in fact, hurried and, finally, a drag.

Still, he dusted himself with baby powder and dabbed the athlete's foot between his two smallest toes with a cotton-wad soaked in alcohol, denatured. Both feet. Toenails needed cutting here and there, but he didn't do it.

Back in his bedroom he stood, naked, washed and dusted, in a bar of sunlight streaming in, and loaded his miniature pipe (with tiny curved mouthpiece) full and tamped. The grass was almost black, and sticky. He turned toward the sunlight as he lit and drew. Full lung-full held tight and extra air sucked in. Faintest warmth of sun on powdered prick and balls. Hazy rooftop scene through match-stick blinds. Silk! Bare feet on red-brown painted floor, dusty. No matter how you try.

Put the pretty pipe back on table. No waste there, it goes right out, and robe on — raw silk short one, like a page. Yoghurt!

Jimmy Vahey liked fruit and honey and sour things. Pickles and yogurt and sweet things — honey and fruit. Also, the kitchen was perfectly clean. And coffee. Perfect coffee down to the coffee store on Polk, endless mixtures, not really too expensive. He always got hung-up making it in little coffeemakers like two coffeemakers upside down against each other. And eggs in butter in the belgian iron orange-inside frying omelette pan. Blue outside. Surprisingly heavy considering the wooden handle.

Toast! Yellow-pine table needs bleaching again. Too far . . .

So Jimmy Vahey, too far, reaches for the brandy bottle and waits through a cup of coffee finally made to perfection, with brandy in it, till back again and frying eggs.

•   •   •   •   •   •   •

Linda Vahey comes through the door with lots of key-rattling and stooping to pick up packages which, while opening the door, had to be put down on the door-stoop. Also, she has a cigarette in her mouth which bothers her eyes the while. And a large leather purse like a saddlebag.

All this equipment is finally brought into the living room and put on the marble-slab coffee table, on bricks, — except for the cigarette which is put out in the lava-rock mexican ash tray (originally a corn-grinder). The purse remains in the living room, on the floor beside the marble-slab table, but the paper bag is brought into the kitchen where Jimmy Vahey is frying, or basting, his eggs. In butter.

They kiss.

"These eggs are beautiful. Where did you get them?"

"Chinatown, look at what I got just now."

"Wait a minute. They're done."

Jimmy Vahey perfectly slides the eggs onto a blue-and-white thick china plate they bought at the Good Will. The eggs are lightly dusted with paprika, salt and pepper. At this very instant two slices of toast spring up from the toaster.

Jimmy Vahey puts the plate of eggs down on the yellow-pine table and places a slice of toast on each side of the plate — the toast resting on the table and leaning against the sides of the plate. The butter is there, on another blue-and-white plate. Into a thick blue-and-white mug he pours perfect coffee and adds, from the swell-bottomed long-necked bottle, a little brandy. All the silverware is there, the napkin is there, he sits in yellow-pine chair and says:

"All right. What?"

Linda Vahey takes out of the paper bag, now on the table, a bolt of cloth — or, at least, a part of a bolt. The cloth is dull moss-green with regular geometric brown figures — small pattern as in a man's tie.

"I thought I'd make scallopy curtains on brass rods

for the windows, the bottom halves, in the living room."

Jimmy Vahey, eating, says:

"Very pretty. Really, very pretty."

Looking at the cloth with total absorption, Linda Vahey says:

"Yes."

Then she goes into the living room and holds the cloth against the bottom windows. Jimmy Vahey eats, his back toward her, and finally begins to plan his day.

"I started a pipe in the bedroom."

"O.K.," still holding up, and looking at, the cloth.

She gets up and goes into the bedroom. Jimmy Vahey realizes he needs another cup of coffee, but no more brandy. Pours himself some coffee, and thinks about jazz: Sonny Rollins at the Workshop. Think I'll dig Sonny Rollins at the Workshop.

"Think I'll dig Sonny Rollins at the Workshop, want to come along?" yelling it, so she'll hear, way off in the bed-room.

Linda Vahey comes out of the bedroom holding her breath, she can't talk, so only shakes her head for "No." The pipe is in her hand. She walks up to Jimmy and gives him the pipe, lets out her breath, and kisses him on the forehead.

"No. You go. I've got these curtains and Marilyn is coming over to pose."

Jimmy Vahey, his arm around Linda's waist, he sitting and she standing, draws on the pipe and, while holding his breath, snuggles his head against her slender tummy. She absently strokes his hair while looking out the kitchen window — thinking about the funny shapes of chimney-pots and wondering where you could buy them: good for garden lamps & much, much, cheaper.

A real good grab at the back of his head he sees the pipe at the end of his hand against the yellow-pine table. Top.

"O.K.," he says, "I'll go alone."

Not at all bugged, you understand, really meaning the "O.K."

·   ·   ·   ·   ·   ·   ·

In soft light the living room with Linda Vahey measuring cloth and windows, Jimmy Vahey still walking around, or sitting, in his raw silk short japanese robe that comes just below his genitals — legs bare and barefooted.

Marilyn enters about 5 o'clock: a very pretty very thin short girl, a small girl, almost no breasts at all and a vogue face without, voguishly, any make-up, except eye make-up. While she and Linda talk, and Linda starts making something strange and delicious for dinner (out of the contents of the other paper bag she, earlier, brought home), Jimmy Vahey re-enters the bedroom and fixes with Methedrine.

It takes him a long time.

Jimmy Vahey is very careful. He has: an apothecary jar (with buffed stopper) full of sterile cotton already broken up into dab-size hunks, a very expensive hypodermic outfit (for which he has a prescription: diabetic, though he isn't), endless needles all of them sharp, and a large box of ampules of Methedrine arranged like eggs in an egg crate — tiny glass pointy-tipped eggs with little labels on them. He also has a bottle of alcohol and a knitted, black, necktie. Putting all of these things into operation in exactly the right sequence, and finding his vein easily (he does not do this sort of thing often enough to ruin his veins) he shoots an ampule into (not the vein itself this time, changing his mind at the last minute and wanting it to last) the deltoid muscle of his left arm. Nothing happens, as he knows it won't, so he has all this time to put everything away and go back into the living room.

Marilyn is now naked on the couch, Linda is sketching her. The absolute last rays of sunshine are coming goldenly

into the room. The couch is not a couch but a mattress
covered with blue velvet. Many red velvet pillows. Marilyn is
very graceful, white, and bony — the boniness not taking
away from her femininity. Linda sketches intently below her
lank, dyed, red hair. Huge eyes all outlined with make-up.
Four of them. Linda's and Marilyn's. Marilyn has the pipe
in her hand.

Jimmy Vahey gets hit by the shot just as he smells the
dinner — some kind of creamed meat — cooking. He gets a
short take that Marilyn is evil (seeing her staring at Linda-
while-she-draws like Salome-where-she-danced, and Arizona)
and realizes that he must eat though he won't want to — and
to do this should have a little pot.

Jimmy Vahey gets up and walks toward Marilyn to take
the pipe from out her hand — she doesn't even look up, just
stares and stares at Linda drawing her — and decides to stand
right there and look directly at her narrow snatch while
taking his toke. Narrow. The hairs folding in. The crease so
innocent and small. Voracious mouth. Tiny mouth like face-
mouth, really, but so seen. Eating.

Much too far, and wrong. So:

Back in the bedroom for goofball. Taken in warm water
with thought of port.

Back into kitchen for crystal glass and white port (Ital-
ian Swiss Colony) to return to room. Marijuana now taking
over the scene is lovely. The girls good friends. The port in
hand. The light failing.

"Shall I turn on the light?"

"Yes, sweety," not looking up from the drawing.

Jimmy Vahey gets all involved with lighting. The girls
continue staring at each other — the one to draw, the other
to watch drawer drawing. Her. Suddenly the light is exactly
right.

Three people pleased.

Jimmy Vahey, proud of lighting, lights and smokes and
passes the pipe to Marilyn, who accepts the pipe with a daz-
zling and real little smile and eye flash. Naked. Look to
Linda to see her face is down, finger smudging shading of
drawing, to:
Dinner!
Jimmy Vahey taking over the kitchen. Creamed meat
going fine. Salad chopped not dressing. Jimmy Vahey with
many oil bottles. And vinegar. Jimmy Vahey announcing
a dressing. Jimmy Vahey considering table-set. And candles.
Girls giggle. Signal. "He's stoned" signal. Not to him.
Suddenly all three eating a most delicious meal!
Jimmy Vahey witty. Marilyn all broken up and most del-
icately beautiful in Linda's robe. Linda even more beautiful,
though not so delicate, good, those better hips thighs.
But not together. Don't push it. Linda drawing. Linda
making curtains. Off. Off to Sonny Rollins.
"Now you wash the dishes sweety though I promised
myself, if not you, I'd do them and put this kitchen back
exactly where it beautifully is most of the time — Marilyn I
want you to know exactly how I deeply appreciate this
gorgeous broad of mine, as you know, who — *not only* so
beautifully draws and paints and even, I must admit, gets
most of the bread to run this house, — but WHO — as well
you understand, is so sweetly mine (and yours too, but in
another, or did I double-think just then?, way?) but no. I
have to go immediately as planned to hear Sonny Rollins the
great Sonny as planned while you two figure all those girl-
scenes out you so sweetly talk all day. Curtains. Yes."
And so saying, Jimmy Vahey prepared to dress for
Sonny Rollins only ten blocks down the street. Knowing,
of course, too far . . .

in another direction entirely

Took two goofballs smelled his pits and took another, better, shower.

Standing in the tiny room solid steam he studied, through the small hole he kept wiping in the mirror, his tidy beard: clump of hair on chin like, but not, a Vandyke. Wondering about Marilyn. Back into bedroom to fill another pipe (not the one still downstairs with the girls). Port occurred to him again, and Raga. Not downstairs, in the kitchen, same floor.

Into the living room to put a long Raga on the phonograph. Not Hi-Fi. That worried him.

The Raga was the one with unbearable long drum passage before the sitar finally comes in (with such relief, having been teased and teased, in). Back, the bathroom wasn't near so steamy. Wiped off the mirror. A whole mirror now. Small scissors clipping impeccable beard. Raga. Almost almost.

So, back to the bedroom the sure last twist of the final dial: one more long and oh so languorous toke on the finest of all pipes — standing by the window looking through silk-wood at now blue and neon night sky. There!

He dressed from four sport shirts laid out, all of them perfectly ironed, on the bed and knife-crease slacks, his beard perfect with tiny curved scissors. Calming, the lady-talk from kitchen and plate-clank. All-slow. Light just right with candle to see shirt by. Ivy the league of strip. Brown and blue stripe impossible combination only a few years back now buyable everywhere. We are winning! Shitty-green in all $300 a suit-store. Slower.

Sip on the port glass. Play small pattern on Marimba now Raga gone and Linda turned it off. What a woman. I have!

Perfect.

Into the living room. Empty. Marilyn gone and Linda at work on 6 by 8 foot canvas mostly white paint mixing her colors so.

"How do I look?" he said.

"Beautiful" kissing him, and right back, though the whole thing was superbly warm as the door closed behind him and he, in his fresh pressed gabardine zipper jacket, crease-slack, ivy-shirt, hair combed (short) and clip-beard, walked down steep steep cement hill in balmy air toward the last set (it now being midnight) of Sonny Rollins . . . to enter the place too dark for his shades so he took them off and heard, actually heard, each note . . .

Noting the bunch of hair Sonny wore under, not on, the chin and his long wait between notes so he, Jimmy Vahey, could only help to hear.

One set. Four numbers in four and every complete tempo and all the keys. One scotch before him, twiddling it.

Heard every note and came back. Perfect. Impeccable and groomed the groom returning.

To watch her, his Linda, painting. Hours and hours without a comment till suddenly, but not all all at once, they saw they were once again together.

And made it so.

[*Evergreen Review*, No. 17, March-April 1961]

THE LATE URBAN LOVE OF PETER HELD

Peter Held was a tall thin man with regular, unremarkable, features. He wore glasses and gray double-breasted shark-skin suits. His black shoes were neither shined nor in need of one. He always carried a newspaper and he never wore a hat.

Peter Held worked for a featureless little company with offices in the garment district of New York City. He was an accountant and always did his work blamelessly and on time.

He lived in a single furnished room in the West 70s, just off Central Park. His room had bland tan wallpaper and spackled brown-and-yellow linoleum rugs. There was a brown radio on top of his dresser.

The radio was always on when Peter Held was in his room. He'd sit in his wicker rocking chair reading the evening paper and listening to classical music, until finally daylight failed and it was too dark to read. Then he'd sit for a while with only the small yellow light from the radio dial. Then he'd get up, turn on the light, put on his coat, turn off the radio and the light, and go out to a same small restaurant to eat his dinner. Walking soundlessly down the dusty carpeted stairs of the narrow brownstone house. Out through the frosted-glass doors. Down the brownstone steps. Onto the street. Under the street lights.

The only interesting thing about Peter Held is a very interesting thing indeed, and explains everything else about him. Peter Held was 42 years old at the time of this story and he had never, even in the slightest way, been in love. Then, when he was 42 years old, he did fall in love — it happened to him strangely, and by accident, and it very nearly ruined his life.

It is important to understand how deeply Peter Held had never been in love. It was not just that he never had anyone up to his little room. Nor was it a matter of something, out of shyness or fear, which he denied himself. There had been nothing in his whole life that could have given to anyone the idea that Peter Held felt himself to be missing out on something. Instead you got the idea there was something missing from *him* — a strange blank in his very nature.

Never in his life had he felt so much as a troublesome twinge from the forces that drive us all. Even as a boy he was spared the torments of being a Son to a Mother. He got plenty of petting and loving from Mother and Aunts (but stood coldly the while, turning his head as if in annoyance, but not in annoyance, away). And now, when we find him, his presence in his office was strange and transparent — those who worked with him could scarcely remember whether he'd been there that day — and none of the secretaries felt he was either handsome or not, exciting or dull, shy or hostile, or anything else.

Once in a while somebody new in the office would sit beside Peter Held at coffee, and she would always (it was almost magical the way it always happened) ask him if he wasn't lonely. He'd always ponder the question and then say "no" as one would say to a question he didn't understand, but wished to get out of the way because, and only because, of its remoteness.

Now the room that Peter Held lived in looked out onto a small coutyard, not really a back yard — a space left over and in between the buildings that formed his block. Two larger brick apartment buildings hedged in Peter Held's building and the similar brownstone building across the way. So what was left was a small area walled in on every side and towered over by two large buildings — while two smaller, brownstone, buildings closed it in, back to back. This small area was paved with concrete and had many city trees in it: "Stink Trees."

"Stink Trees" is not the right name, but that is the name Peter Held knew them by. Once he asked a man what kind of trees they were: those trees that grow in cities and seem to be able to grow anywhere, without light or air, even at times pushing up through the cracking sidewalks. "Stink Trees," the man said. "That's a funny name," said Peter Held, "Why do you call them Stink Trees?" And the man said, "I don't know, except maybe they reproduce all the time and are very messy."

So these trees grew in such a way that Peter Held, whose top-floor room looked out over this courtyard, had almost perfect privacy. All he could see from his single window was part of the wall across the way, and the tops of a lot of stink trees. The part of the wall he could see had a single window in it. So here was Peter Held in the center of the world's largest city with such perfect privacy that, when it was dark and everybody turned the lights on, all he could see was a square of light from a single window 75 feet away. All the rest was city-lit sky and huge, windowless, brick walls and stink-tree tops.

For years and years the people who lived behind the window across the way had been an elderly couple with habits as simple and decorous as Peter Held's. Then the couple moved. The blinds were taken down, the furniture was removed, and for nearly a week the room across the way was empty. Peter Held could see wallpaper, very like his own, and part of a doorway. Then a young girl moved in and began fixing the place up, and Peter Held fell gradually in love with her.

Peter Held came home, turned on his radio (softly, so as not to bother his neighbors), sat in his wicker rocking

chair, and began reading his newspaper. In the room across
the way he could see a blond girl in jeans and white, man's,
shirt. She was climbing up and down a ladder, painting
the wallpaper with flat white paint. She couldn't have been
over 20 and she might have been as young as 18. She was
chunkily built and not particularly pretty. She was just a
young blond girl with a painting-roller in her hand. Up and
down and moving a ladder.

But, like all girls this age who are reasonably healthy,
she had the fresh and simple beauty that is standard for it
all. Grace. Movement and complexion brief in time, beyond
all fashions and prettiness. Uncopyable by women. Supplied
by mind to all his later loves by men . . .

Peter Held read his paper, more or less aware of the
music from his radio and the girl across the way, and, as
the light began to fail, dozed off. The image of the girl
across the way grew brighter as the day became more dim,
until finally the square of light from her window sat brightly
in a ground of almost total darkness. And Peter Held received
this changing image half in dream and half within reality as
he dozed in his wicker rocking chair, his paper on his lap.

Then he found himself in a dark room, awake, without
having planned any of it, watching the girl undress.

Either she didn't know anyone could look into her
blindless window, or she didn't care. But there she was:
standing before her window, taking her shirt off, removing
her jeans, then, standing very close to the window (arms-
behind back, hands fiddling up high between her shoulder
blades) she removed her brassiere.

Leaning slightly forward she slid the brassiere over her
arms and, brassiere still in one hand, put both her hands on
the windowsill and stared down into the courtyard — breasts
swinging almost imperceptibly back and forth, as if to cool
them. Then she turned and walked directly away from him,
stopped in the center of the room, and slipped down plain

white panties off her chunky rump and thighs. Naked, she examined her body here and there and finally walked away from Peter Held's unwilling eyes.

Fascinated, embarrassed, and annoyed, he lowered his window shade, turned on his light, put on his coat, turned off his light and his radio, and went out to dinner. When he returned he raised his blind almost fearfully and was relieved to see that the window across the way was dark.

He lowered his blind, undressed, turned out his light, raised the blind again, and went to bed dressed in flannel pajamas. While he slept, with the radio softly playing as was his habit, he was aware, or dreamed, that the light across the way kept going on and off.

●   ●   ●   ●   ●   ●   ●

That was the beginning. But it kept going on that way until a form began to show — an almost mystic union or display which Peter Held finally became unable to withstand.

He'd come home and deliberately try to avoid her. He moved his chair so the back of it was to the window. But he liked the last evening light, so kept the window-blind up. Then, when light finally failed and he'd go to lower the blind, there she'd be: standing in a white cotton slip, bare to the waist, combing.

Leaning out of her window, looking down, her hair thrown goldenly, she combed and brushed, stopping now and then to watch what may have been the alley cats criss-crossing the cement below. Then toss of hair behind her and perfect rise of her breasts as her hands and arms were raised to fluff her hair that way. Deep cut of her navel just above her simple slip. Then off with the slip and peasant glow of buttocks to Peter's caught and accidental eye . . .

It got uncanny and Peter Held not only finally stopped trying to give it up — he actually included it within his little

day. Testing, he once turned his light off, raised the blind
twice, settled in his wicker chair, and: on went the light
across the way, up went the blind, and on she came — dif-
ferently, as always, always doing something naturally a part
of her day, always seeming unaware of her almost certainly
invisible audience.

It got to be a need. The few days they didn't meet
would upset Peter Held in a way he couldn't relate to anything he'd ever known. He'd come home from work and
fiddle through the paper, glancing out the window from
time to time. He never rushed it. Then, when it was dark
enough, he'd go through what was now the ritual: light off,
blind up and down twice, then settle in the wicker chair.
To gaze on darkness a while, or on the square of light of
her window-shade, and usually to see the blind go up re-
vealing whatever show was his to see that night. Once in a
rare while nothing would happen. But usually something
did, and if it did, it was oddly timed to his blind-raises.

Until, to test it even further, he turned his light on,
then off, then raised the window blind twice, at 5 o'clock
in the morning. Then sat in his chair, this time naked since
he'd run out of clean pajamas. And sure enough, on came
the light (though there was some delay) and she rose in a
simple country nightgown, hair all loosened from her usual
ponytail, yawned, and then began to sway. Back and forth,
rocking on her hip joints, hands rubbing at her eyes. Then
slipped the nightgown over her head and, almost glowering
directly at him under lowered eyebrows, continued to rock
upon her hips, hands cupped behind each cheek of rump,
shoving her mounded golden triangle directly out, out the
window, toward old Peter Held.

How could he explain it? What could he possibly do?
He thought of moving several times (in the morning, in the
subway, on his way to work) but by nightfall always re-
jected the idea. Images he'd never seen kept passing between

him and the numbers he worked on in his columned and
accurate books. Once he picked up a typing eraser the girl
next to him dropped — and she was pleased and suprised
when he shyly handed it back to her. He noticed the receptionist's pointy shoes. And when he told her (sort of) one
day, he blushed at her little reply.

It all got broken and strange. Peter Held, for the first
time in his life, got nervous about schedules and other little
things. For example, he'd think: "Think I'll eat my lunch in
Central Park." He'd have to hurry, get a hot-dog, and a car-
ton of milk. Go to the park (by bus), get an empty place
on a bench. Eat. Then sit, worrying about having to go back
to the office, letting the sun strike his face. All the sounds
came in: roller skates on broken pavement, squeals, thrum
of auto-sounds, tap of cane and far-away calling of people's
names.

So that, opening his eyes again, Peter Held noticed
that every place on the benches in Central Park was filled.
Hundreds of people sat, like him, on the long benches that
curve along the paths in Central Park. And in that first good
sun of April all the faces were lifted, eyes closed, toward the
sun. As the sun moved the faces turned, like flowers, turning
as the sun turned. And, for the first time in his life, Peter
Held felt lonely.

•   •   •   •   •   •   •

He was finally like a thing in a trance, and captive. All
he could think of all day was when could he see his girl. She
almost never denied him, always answered, or seemed to
answer, his helplessly given signal — which he performed
more and more gracefully as time went on, though it clearly
was something foolish, unreal, and something which could
never work.

But it worked. Even on the day he came home early,

sick with it, and took off his clothes (as now he always did), made the signal, and settled in his chair to love. She came to him that hot afternoon as naturally as ever — sat nude on her windowsill and looked, with closed eyes, up to the sun. For a long, long, time. Motionless.

It was that very day that Peter Held resolved to meet her. It came to him first as a furtive little idea, and then suddenly he realized he'd really decided long before — it was now only a matter of tactics, not a decision at all. But how to do it?

He considered flowers, but saw himself at her door, 42 years old with flowers, like an old roué, without a way to begin his conversation. He thought of a book. He thought of witty opening remarks. But finally his essential sanity prevailed, and he decided to drive through everything and just appear — as simply as she'd appeared to him. He'd just introduce himself. He'd just get up to that door and knock and introduce himself and let whatever happened happen.

It took some doing for a person as shy as Peter Held to realize this was the only way. But he realized it. And he did it, or almost did it.

He phoned his office pretending sickness for the first time in his life, ate a good breakfast, and took a walk in Central Park. His excitement mounted as he walked about and, he was pleased to find, his strength definitely began to rise to meet his task. When he left the park and strode toward her door he felt strong, if giddy and very humble indeed.

To arrive at a new brass door on a new front of an old brownstone building. To enter. To see in a small hallway a dozen brass mail-box lids set in slabs of marble. To see a further brass and very locked door. To realize he didn't even know her name! And to turn numbly and defeated through the big brass door, out, onto the sunlit, strangely busy, street.

All through that intolerable afternoon he went over it again and again, sitting in his wicker rocking chair, drinking slowly from a bottle of very good brandy — the only liquor he enjoyed. He tried to make sense of what had happened to him. He couldn't face his window. He kept seeing the fine full hips of the receptionist and blocked this image at once, seeing it as confusing and irrelevant to his terrible problem. He got good and drunk.

Peter Held, drunk, opened his window and leaned out, frankly staring at the window across the way. Above the stink trees. In the hot afternoon. He almost called to her. He didn't. Instead he deliberately refrained from making the signal: two times up and down, then seat yourself (naked), and wait. He fell upon his bed face down, and went to sleep.

It was night when he woke up, with a very bad head-ache and a very dry mouth. He wandered through his room getting a glass, filling it from the wash basin, and stood be-fore his window, drinking deliciously cold water. And then it happened.

Without his signal, her window-blind went up.

This had never happened since the very first times he saw her. And now she raised her blind, lowered it, raised it again. Peter Held stood terrified, the glass of water in his hand. He saw her turn and run toward her door. The door opened and a young man came in, closed the door behind him, and very confidently took the girl into his arms. While they kissed she reached back for the string on the window blind and lowered it. That was the last time Peter Held beheld his love. No amount of signalling ever called her back again.

And the loneliness he had only recently come to know became the only and overwhelming thing in Peter's rudely expanding life. His apartness from the roller-skating children, the carriage-pushing women, the selling, alert, loud little men with carts of vegetables who knew all the gossip in the block — his strangeness, even, from the other tenants in the house where he'd lived for nearly 15 years, all these became cruel and present and *there*. So he talked to the man he always bought his paper from. And overtipped his waitress.

He couldn't sleep, but kept a futile vigil in his wicker chair, signalled and signalled, almost all night long. Then, almost in anger, he'd walk in Central Park at 3 and 4 in the morning — to be accosted by bleached fairies with Afghan dogs on silver chains, among scuttering coated shapes that followed a while and then dipped off along other paths, under icy summer streetlights above the empty green benches in Central Park.

To work, with burned eyes and shakey fingers and co-workers worrying about his health.

Till finally it loosened its hold upon him. It was very gradual, almost as slow as his love had grown. But it dwindled. In about a month he'd forget to make the signal now and then. After that, whole weeks would pass without the need to even glance across the way. The park got bearable again — children a nuisance and the terrors of late-park wanderers dimly remembered and easy to avoid.

Visions such as that about faces of people, the sun, and flowers, ceased to trouble him or to occur.

Until, after not so many months really, everything went back to be exactly the way it was before.

And Peter Held was never lonely again.

CODA

"That's just beautiful, Leo, does it mean what I think it does? I mean, for us?"

"If you want to."

"I'll do it, but I don't think I want to. I mean, sure, I guess you're my man, and if you think that's the way it is, I'll go, but I have this feeling about who are we? Are you, we, writing the novel or is the novel writing us?

"Both."

"What I'm trying to say is, you write this book and chapter by chapter I hear you read it to me, and it's true, like you talk about true, the way a plumb-bob is true, but is there really anywhere else to go?

"Wouldn't it be pretty to think so."

"Somebody else already said that."

"And the other guy had somebody rowing a boat all the way to Sweden, and you wonder what in the world is there in Sweden, and the whole thing falls apart into some kind of cop-out. Doesn't it? Honey, I really mean this, I really mean I want to go the rest of the way with you, and I know we can do it, but I don't trust that ending, that ending of the book, I mean, the whole back of the beat routine, and the final finger at the vulgar bastard, here, somehow, some God Damned way . . ."

"Ah baby I didn't mean to put your book down, it's beautiful, it's just perfect that way, and . . ."

"FORGET IT!" Leo, suddenly leaping from the bed's edge, raging, his fists tight, swinging at nothing: "It's the same dumb thing! It's what I almost learned in the mountains! You gotta have *some* good men in the mountains!

137

And the Cities! (And then, not wanting to frighten her,
seeing her start to cringe, as she did, watching his rages
and hurting so, herself, seeing his futile pain, he caught
himself short, sat down beside her, and held her, and
laid her head upon his lap, and almost absently stroked
her hair as he, still raging, but subsiding, tried to get back.
  "Forget it! Forget it! Forget it! Only I WILL NOT
forget it! I WON'T! I WON'T!" (The only thing stopping
another insane pounding of some table till his right hand
broke its bones again, and nothing accomplished at all, the
only thing stopping all this, his love for her, and the strength
he gained by touching her, his hand become strong, instead
of foolish, by stroking her soft, so vulnerable, hair), he gradually became almost articulate again.
  "Look, the real thing is to stay home and take it. It's
like that Chinaman who said 'the brush may paint the mountains and rivers though the territory is lost,' remember that?"
  "Sure, baby, sure," putting her hand on the hand that
stroked her hair.
  "And what I almost learned in the mountains, that
poem I just can't finish 'cause I don't understand it yet, is the
same thing. You have to come back. Like the Bodhisattva.
Avalokiteshvara. Or put it simply: somebody has to bandage
the wounded. I cannot be free if my nation suffers so, no not
my nation, my Tribe! I can't just prophesy the doom of my
Tribe, and then split, and say 'I told you so.' I don't know
why, but I really do know I can't, I won't, I'm just going to
stay here and take it. Like William Carlos Williams did, or
like Whalen's poem: 'an embarrassment, like the buffalo, the
Indian, like Yellowstone National Park!' Excuse me, I gotta
blow my nose."
  Leo carefully unentangled himself from the now quite
complicated hand on stroking hand and head on lap arrange-
ment, rose from the bed's edge, found the kleenex, blew his
nose and washed his face in the garage at the sink. Since he

was already there, anyway, he took a piss. All this gave him
time to clear his lungs in long breaths and heavy whooshes
of air, out.

He then snorted his nose, clean, into the sink, ran water
to wash the phlegm away, and cleaned his nose with finger
and water. Then he dried his previously tear-wet, nose-
draining, face, and re-entered his room.

By now she was undressed, tucked in bed, and worried.

"I'm sorry, baby, I don't mean to come on that way, but
the whole thing is too much sometimes." Undressed, and got
in bed beside her.

"I thought it was just because I didn't like the way the
book ended."

"That's why I keep you around, to keep my head
straight."

Familiar cuddling maneuvers got their bodies arranged
just right. All tensions vanished. He kissed her on the neck and
she, her back to him, and he, holding both her breasts, moved
her buttocks to the exact warming position against his belly,
his thighs, and what might or might not be his rising, other,
need.

"I really meant that, baby, it does mean that for you and
me, that we go off together, 'cause I can't do it alone anymore, and then, as we've been saying, it looks like we stick it
out, here, and . . ."

"This will probably break the mood, and everything,
but I can't help wondering how the book will end."

"Like this."

GREY FOX PAPERBACKS:

Allen Ginsberg: *The Gates of Wrath:*
Rhymed Poems 1948-1952

Interview with Allen Young

Lew Welch: *Collected Correspondence*

How I Work as a Poet
& Other Essays / Plays / Stories

Ring of Bone: Collected Poems 1950-1971

Trip Trap: Haiku along the road from
San Francisco to New York in 1959.
With Jack Kerouac & Albert Saijo

Philip Whalen: *Scenes of Life at the Capital*